comparative
RELIGION

Investigate the World Through Religious Tradition

INQUIRE AND INVESTIGATE

Carla Mooney
Illustrated by Lena Chandhok

Nomad Press
A division of Nomad Communications
10 9 8 7 6 5 4 3 2 1

This book was manufactured by Marquis Book Printing,
Montmagny, Québec, Canada
October 2015, Job #115364
ISBN Softcover: 978-1-61930-305-8
ISBN Hardcover: 978-1-61930-301-0

Illustrations by Lena Chandhok
Educational Consultant, Marla Conn

Questions regarding the ordering of this book should be addressed to
Nomad Press
2456 Christian St.
White River Junction, VT 05001
www.nomadpress.net

Printed in Canada.

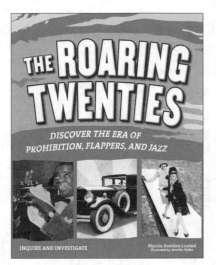

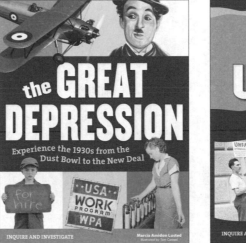

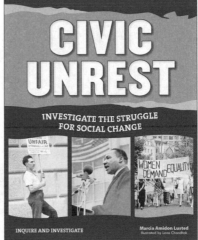

Social studies titles in the
Inquire and Investigate series

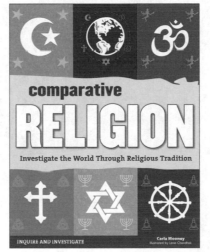

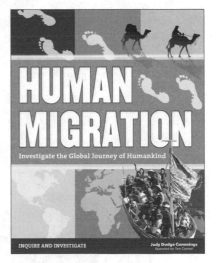

You can use a smartphone or tablet app to scan the QR codes and explore more about religion! Cover up neighboring QR codes to make sure you're scanning the right one. You can find a list of each URL on the Resources page.

If the QR code doesn't work, try searching the Internet with the Keyword Prompts to find other helpful sources.

Contents

TIMELINE

circa 2000 BCE.......... Abraham, considered the father of the Jewish religion, lives in the Middle East.

1300 BCE .... Moses leads the Israelites from Egypt to Canaan and receives the Torah and commandments from God.

1200–900 BCE .... The four Vedas are written, the oldest Hindu sacred texts.

Sixth century BCE .... The first of the Hindu Upanishads is written.

586 BCE .... The Babylonians conquer the Israelites and destroy the First Temple of Jerusalem.

563 BCE .... Siddhartha Gautama, who would become known as Buddha, is born.

Fifth century BCE ..... Branches of Buddhism emerge as the religion spreads across Asia.

Third century BCE .... India's Emperor Asoka converts to Buddhism.

First century BCE...... The Pali Canon, a collection of Buddha's teachings, are written down.

First century BCE...... The Temple of Jerusalem is rebuilt by King Herod. It is later destroyed by the Romans in 70 CE.

4 CE .... Jesus is born. Christians believe him to be the Son of God.

30–36 CE .... Jesus is crucified by the Romans. Christians believe that he rises from the dead three days later and ascends to heaven.

313........................... The Roman emperor Constantine issues the Edict of Milan, which allows Christianity to be practiced freely.

392........................... Christianity is declared to be the religion of the Roman Empire.

Hinduism
The four Vedas are written.

Judaism
Moses is in danger from Pharaoh's men.

Buddhism
Buddha is born and

vi

610............................ The prophet Muhammad receives his first revelation from God, which becomes the Qur'an, the sacred text of Islam.

632............................ Muhammad and his followers conquer the city of Mecca.

632............................ Muhammad dies. Muslims disagree on who should succeed him as leader, resulting in the two branches of Islam, Sunni and Shi'a.

1054............................ The Great Schism occurs, dividing Christianity into the Roman Catholic and Eastern Orthodox branches.

1095–1291............... A series of Crusades are launched by the Catholic Church to retake Jerusalem from the Muslims.

Third century........... Buddhism spreads in China.

1391............................ The first Dalai Lama, the spiritual leader of Tibet and Buddhists, is born.

Nineteenth century... Different branches of Judaism—Reform, Orthodox, and Conservative—emerge.

1935............................ The 14th Dalai Lama is born.

1938–1945............... Millions of Jews are killed during the Holocaust in Nazi Germany.

1948............................ The state of Israel is founded in the Middle East, leading to a series of conflicts between Israel and Islamic states.

1989............................ The Dalai Lama receives the Nobel Prize for Peace for his efforts to negotiate peace between Tibet and China.

2013............................ Father Jorge Mario Bergoglio becomes Pope Francis, the leader of the Catholic Church.

...uches blossoms.

Christianity
Jesus is born in a manger.

Islam
Muhammad is born in hill country.

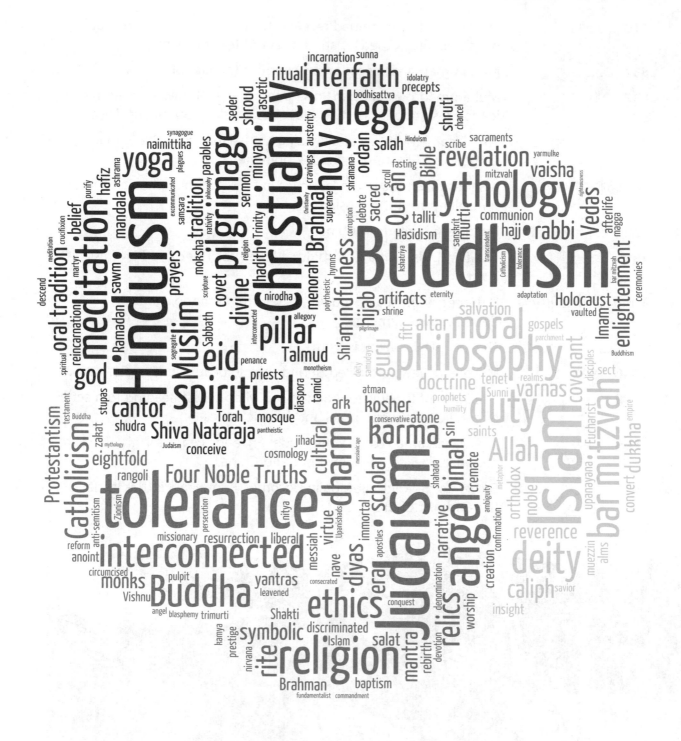

Introduction

What Is Religion?

What influence does religion have on our lives?

Different people have different definitions of religion. But most people agree that religion is a set of beliefs about the cause, nature, and purpose of the universe based on the teachings of a spiritual leader.

Around the world, the majority of people say that they are religious. This is just as true today as it was in the past. Yet religion means many things to many people. A Muslim or a Jewish person might define religion differently from a Buddhist or a Christian or a person who follows the Hindu faith. Even within religious traditions there can be differences in beliefs. There have been countless religions in human history and each has its own distinct beliefs and rituals.

Whether we are religious or not, manifestations of religion exist all around us. These can be seen in ceremonies and rituals and in a variety of moral and ethical codes of behavior.

Religion is a powerful force in our world. It is the foundation of a wide range of moral values and cultural identities. These values and identities often influence and guide the behavior and choices of many people.

> In some cases, religion also influences the actions of entire nations. Directly or indirectly, religion affects all of our lives.

So what exactly is religion? You probably know it when you see it, but most people have a hard time defining it. The concept of religion includes a wide variety of doctrines, rituals, forms, leaders, and stories. One broad definition of religion is a set of beliefs about the cause, nature, and purpose of the universe.

RELIGIONS AROUND THE WORLD

While there are many religions around the world, the majority of people identify with one of the five major religions: Hinduism, Judaism, Buddhism, Christianity, and Islam. These religions have some similarities, but they also have many differences. For example, some religions are polytheistic, meaning that followers worship many gods. Others are monotheistic—members believe in one supreme god.

In addition, there are significant differences in how each religion addresses the idea of afterlife. Those who follow the Hindu faith believe that the soul is reborn over and over again, while Christians believe in an eternal heaven or hell.

Most of the major religions have common elements, such as a belief in some type of deity or supreme being. They also present a code of conduct that guides people in how to live their lives. These religions usually also have a doctrine of salvation, or a way for followers to be forgiven for their transgressions.

I LIKE TO THINK OF REINCARNATION AS RECYCLING FOR YOUR SOUL!

Have you ever been to a church service or made a pilgrimage to a holy site? Most of the world's religions have specific ways in which followers observe their faith. These can include religious rituals, ceremonies, prayers, meditation, music, and feasting or fasting. Observing a faith often involves using physical items or spaces, such as artifacts, places of worship, or relics.

Most major religions also have central stories that explain the answers to different questions. How did the world begin? Where did humans come from? How were gods created? A religion's stories often include a creation story, which explains how the world and all of its creatures, including people, originated. Stories can also include a history of the faith's gods, prophets, and other important figures.

> Many stories or parables illustrate the beliefs and values of the religion. This narrative can be an oral tradition or a set of scriptures.

Every major faith has a collection of sacred texts, such as the Christian Bible and the Muslim Qur'an. These sacred books detail the faith's central ideals. They narrate the history of the religion and its traditions. In many cases, these sacred texts are believed to have been given to followers by a supreme deity.

In addition to sacred texts, many religions have other texts that explain their philosophy and doctrine. Often these texts detail the rules of conduct that followers are expected to obey. For example, in the Jewish and Christian faiths, the Ten Commandments are rules that followers strive to live by.

EXPLORING RELIGION'S SIMILARITIES AND DIFFERENCES

Comparative Religion: Investigate the World Through Religious Tradition examines the five major religions—Hinduism, Judaism, Buddhism, Christianity, and Islam. This book will help you better understand religion and how it affects different people. We'll examine the religions in this order, from oldest to youngest.

The text and activities in *Comparative Religion* will encourage you to explore both the similarities and the differences among these five religions by comparing and contrasting how each religion addresses the core elements of faith. You will also investigate their cultural, geographic, and spiritual foundations.

Even within the same religion, there are many different practices. Some religious followers believe that traditional teachings are to be followed word for word. Others understand texts as metaphors or lessons. It is always important to be respectful of peoples' beliefs. Ask lots of questions and listen carefully and respectfully to what others have to say.

By understanding the similarities and differences between the world's religions, you will gain a better understanding of how these beliefs unite and divide people around the world.

KEY QUESTIONS

- How does religion help people? Does it ever hurt people?
- Why do so many people follow a religion?
- How is religion related to history? What effects do the different religions have on each other?

HINDU CREATION STORY

Each major religion has a creation story. A creation story explains how the world began and how people and creatures came to live in it. One of the ways to study different religions is to compare the similarities and differences of their creation stories. Watch this video to learn a Hindu creation story.

🔍 Hindu creation story

WHAT IS RELIGION?

Defining religion can be a difficult task. Often, our definition of religion is shaped by our family, experiences, traditions, ethnic and cultural backgrounds, and many other factors. Understanding these influences in your life can be helpful as you compare and contrast the five major religions in this book. Ask a group of friends or classmates to help you explore the definition of religion and discover how different your answers are.

- **For 15 minutes, everyone in the group writes the answer to the following questions.** What is religion? Is there a god? Is there more than one god? How does religion encourage you to behave a certain way?

- **After you have finished writing, each person takes a turn to read out loud what he or she has written.** What similarities did you find in the answers? Were there any central elements that were included in the majority of the answers? How are the answers different?

- **Now go around the group so each person can share a little bit about their personal background and experience with religion.** How do you think their backgrounds affected their answers? How did your background affect your answer? Can you draw any conclusions from your discussion?

...HUH, KNOW WHAT? "JEDI" TOTALLY MEETS OUR CRITERIA.

To investigate more, create a list of criteria that you and your classmates believe are essential to a religion. Why did you include these criteria? Are there any less common religions that you know of that do not meet your criteria? In what ways do faiths other than your own meet your criteria? In what ways do they not meet them?

Chapter 1
Hinduism

What are the rituals, beliefs, teachings, and traditions of Hinduism?

The teachings and traditions of Hinduism have been practiced for thousands of years. Hinduism encompasses many different religious rites and practices.

Hinduism is the oldest of the world's five major religions. Elements of Hinduism have existed for thousands of years. Unlike many other religions, Hinduism does not have a single founder, a single scripture, or a common set of teachings. It does not recognize any one prophet or worship a single god. It does not follow one set of religious rites or traditions.

Instead, Hinduism encompasses a vast number of practices, rituals, beliefs, teachings, and traditions. Hinduism is often described as a family of religions or a way of life.

ORIGINS OF HINDUISM

No specific date marks the beginning of Hinduism. Most people believe that traditions of Hinduism formed in India around 1700 BCE. The word *Hindu* is derived from the River Indus, as is the word *India*. It was used by Muslim invaders in ancient India to identify those people who were native to the Indian subcontinent.

Today, there are about 1 billion Hindus around the world, which is about 15 percent of the world's population. The majority of the people who practice Hinduism live in the South Asia region, primarily in India, Nepal, and Bangladesh.

Although Hinduism includes many different customs and traditions, there are some basic ideas and practices that are shared. Most Hindu traditions believe in a supreme being and in the concepts of truth, dharma, and karma. They also believe in the authority of the Vedas, the sacred scriptures of Hinduism, even though the Vedas are translated differently among traditions.

> Dharma means striving to do the right thing, in accordance with duty and abilities, at all times. According to karma, good actions lead to good reactions, while bad actions lead to negative reactions.

THE FOUR VEDAS

The four Vedas are some of the most ancient sacred texts that exist in the world today. The Vedas contain hymns, incantations, and rituals from Hindu traditions. They also give a view of everyday life in ancient India. On this website, you can explore English translations of the Vedas.

🔍 four Vedas translation

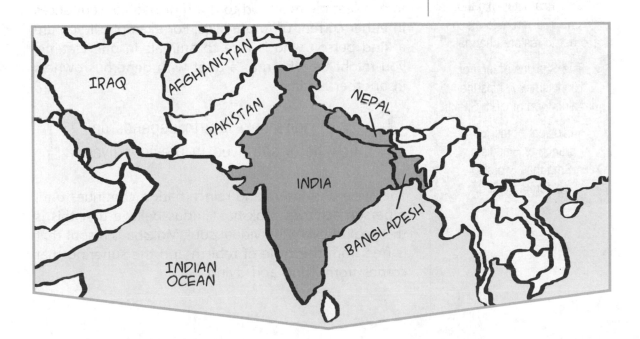

BRANCHES OF HINDUISM

There are several branches of Hinduism, which differ mainly on which form of god each worships.

Shaivas focus on Shiva as the supreme god, in his multiple forms.

Vaishnavas worship Vishnu or his incarnations. Two of Vishnu's most popular incarnations are Krishna, the teacher written about in the Bhagavad Gita, and Rama, the hero of the Ramayana. Vaishnavas believe that God incarnates into the world in different forms in order to restore dharma.

The Shaktas branch of Hinduism worships the feminine form of God, Shakti.

Followers of the fourth branch of Hinduism, Smarthas, worship six forms of God.

THE CYCLE OF REBIRTH

One of the main tenets of Hinduism is the belief in samsara, which is the cycle of birth, death, and rebirth. What do you think happens after we die? Hindus believe that each person has an atman, his or her eternal or real self, which can be thought of as a spirit or soul. An individual soul is immortal and is never created or destroyed—it has always been and always will be. In the continuous cycle of samsara, a person's atman is reborn over and over again.

This process of reincarnation is governed by karma, which is the belief that every action has an equal reaction either immediately or in the future. Karma dictates that good actions lead to positive reactions, while bad actions lead to negative reactions.

In Hinduism, karma exists in a person's current lifetime, and also across several lifetimes. Therefore, an action in one lifetime may lead to good or bad consequences in either current or future lives. For example, if you are a kind person who is nice to animals in one lifetime, you might be reborn as a goat with generous owners in another lifetime.

[A person's next rebirth depends on how he or she lived in previous lives.]

The cycle of samsara and reincarnation continues until a person achieves moksha. Hindus believe that this is the goal of every individual soul. Moksha is a soul that is free from the cycle of rebirth and the suffering that comes from living and dying.

The soul then unites with Brahman, the supreme deity, and realizes its true nature. Several paths can lead to moksha. These include the path of duty, the path of knowledge, and the path of devotion to the gods.

DHARMA

Another key tenet of Hinduism is the concept of dharma. In Hinduism, dharma can be described as duty, virtue, morality, right living, or appropriateness. Dharma is the power that maintains society and the universe. It is the idea that there is an underlying structure and meaning to the world. Behind the complex and random nature of events, there are fundamental principles and an eternal order of things.

Hindus believe that a person can live in harmony with the world and the universe by following that order and structure. Making dharma central to one's life means striving to do the right thing, in accordance with duty and abilities, at all times.

When a person's physical body dies, his or her atman is reborn in a new physical body, which can be human, animal, or a divine being.

At the same time, dharma is a very individual concept. Dharma has different meanings for different people. Every person has obligations and duties based on age, gender, and social position. What is right for a child may not be right for an adult.

To achieve dharma, many Hindus perform rituals and make offerings to the gods to maintain the universe's sense of order. By performing rituals, Hindus believe that they are aligning themselves with the order of the world and becoming one with it.

A SUPREME GOD WITH MANY FORMS

In most Hindu traditions, Brahman is a transcendent power without form and without limit that exists beyond the universe. Everything seen and unseen in the universe is encompassed by Brahman. It is the central force that keeps the endless cycle of creation and destruction moving and is the power that upholds and supports everything in the universe. In this way, Hinduism is a pantheistic religion because it equates God with the universe.

In other ways, Hinduism is also a polytheistic religion that has many gods and goddesses. Most Hindus believe in a supreme god. However, this means different things in different Hindu traditions. In many traditions, the Supreme God has unlimited forms and is represented by many different deities. The different forms appear in Hindu literature as a large number of gods and goddesses.

> The multiple forms of God allow followers to worship in any number of ways, based on their family traditions, community practices, and other influences.

A RULING TRIO

Three Hindu deities have emerged across different Hindu traditions as a ruling trio: Brahma, Vishnu, and Shiva. These three gods form a ruling trio called the Trimurti. Together they are responsible for the creation, maintenance, and destruction of the world.

Brahma is responsible for creation. He created the world and all its creatures. Statues of Brahma show him with four heads, which some people say represent the four Vedas, the ancient sacred texts of Hinduism. Other people believe that Brahma's four heads stand for the four varnas, or social classes, of Hindu society.

The second god is Vishnu, who protects and preserves humanity. Hindus believe that Vishnu returns to Earth during troubled times.

HINDUISM 13

They say that he has been incarnated on Earth nine times, and will return for a tenth incarnation before the end of the world. Some branches of Hinduism worship Vishnu as the only god, or the supreme god. Representations of Vishnu frequently show a human body, blue skin, and four arms.

The third god is Shiva the destroyer. His role is to destroy the universe so he can recreate it. Shiva's powers to destroy the world can also be constructive—by getting rid of the imperfections in this world, he makes space for a better one to be made. In this way, Shiva is seen as the source of both good and evil.

Like Vishnu, Shiva is worshipped by some Hindus as their primary god. Shiva is often shown in images and sculpture as Shiva Nataraja, the Lord of the Dance. Shiva's dance takes place within a circle of flames, representing the ongoing process of birth and death.

SACRED TEXTS

The earliest sacred texts of Hinduism are the four Vedas. The Vedas are a collection of ancient texts that were created during a period of about 1,000 years, beginning around 1200 BCE. The Vedas contain revelations received by ancient scholars and priests. Hindus believe that scholars and priests directly received the texts from God. Because of this, the Vedas are known as *shruti*, meaning "that which is heard."

> Hindus believe that the Vedas have always existed and that when the universe is destroyed, the Vedas will remain.

The Vedas provide the texts, prayers, and instructions for rituals and worship. For hundreds of years, before

DANCING SHIVA

Outside the European Center for Research in Particle Physics (CERN) in Geneva, Switzerland, stands a statue of the dancing Lord Shiva from the Hindu religion. A gift from India, the statue celebrates the association between CERN, where scientists do high-energy physics research, and India.

A plaque next to the statue explains that Lord Shiva danced the universe into existence and will eventually destroy it. For the scientists at CERN, the dancing Shiva portrays the cosmic dance of the subatomic particles they work with every day.

the texts were written down, Hindus passed the texts from one generation to the next by word of mouth. Can you think of other books that began in an oral tradition?

The Vedas include four collections.

- **The Samhitas** are the most ancient part of the Vedas. They include Rig-Veda and consist mostly of hymns of praise to the gods.

- **The Brahmanas** provide instructions for rituals and prayers that guide priests in their duties.

- **The Aranyakas** focus on worship and meditation.

- **The Upanishads** focus on abstract concepts about the nature of the self and the universe.

Other sacred Hindu texts consist of epic poems, which are full of action and stories of the gods. Known as *smriti*, meaning "that which has been remembered," these epic poems explore moral dilemmas and present role models for Hindus to follow.

The Mahabharata tells the story of a war between two royal families and the fight between good and evil. One of the books of the Mahabharata is the Bhagavad Gita, a scripture about virtue and duty. It is written in the form of a dialogue between the prince Arjuna and Krishna, who is an incarnation of the god Vishnu.

In the text, the warrior prince Arjuna is about to go to war against another branch of his family over the question of who should rule the kingdom. Arjuna and his brothers are the rightful heirs, but the other branch of the family took the throne and tried to kill Arjuna and his brothers.

As a member of the warrior class, it is Arjuna's duty to fight. However, he wants to withdraw from the battle because he does not want to kill his family and friends fighting on the other side, which could cause bad karma.

FACTS ON FAITH

SANSKRIT

Sanskrit is the language of Hinduism and Buddhism, as well as Jainism, which is another ancient Indian religion. Sanskrit is also one of India's 22 official languages. Today, Sanskrit is primarily used in Hindu ceremonies, hymns, and mantras. But in some villages of India, the spoken language of Sanskrit is making a comeback.

Arjuna's charioteer, Krishna, advises him to do his duty and fight. He explains to Arjuna that the act of killing only creates bad karma if it is done for the wrong reasons, such as hatred or greed. Doing one's duty, even if it conflicts with personal feelings, is ideal. Krishna also explains that the soul is immortal and death in battle does not mean the end. Only the current body dies, while the soul lives again through reincarnation.

WORSHIP

Unlike many religions, worship in Hinduism is often an individual act. In practice, Hindus are free to choose which deities to worship, whether to worship at home or at a temple, and how often to participate in religious activities.

Many Hindus have a shrine at home where they say prayers, called mantras, and make offerings of water, fruit, flowers, and incense to the deity. A shrine can be a room, a small altar, or a simple picture or statue of the deity, called a murti. Diagrams of the universe, called yantras, might also be used during worship.

The simplest yantra is a circle inside a square inside a rectangle, with four gates that represent the universe's four directions. Hindu temples are based on this design.

> At home, family members often worship together, usually near sunrise and sunset. Hindu worship is called puja.

Hindus decide for themselves when and where they will worship their gods.

Some Hindus worship at temples. The design of a temple is based on the simple yantra described above. In Hindu temples, the parts of the building have symbolic meaning. The central shrine represents the heart of the worshipper, while the temple's tower represents the flight of the spirit to heaven. At the temple, a Hindu priest conducts certain rites with or on the behalf of worshippers. Worshippers may also gather to listen to recitations of the Hindu Epics or participate in a singing of devotionals.

RELIGIOUS RITES

In the Hindu faith, religious rites fall into three categories. Nitya rituals are performed daily. They consist of offerings and prayers made at a home shrine. Naimittika rituals occur at certain times during the year, often to celebrate festivals and give thanks.

Kamya rituals are optional, but highly encouraged. One example of a Kamya ritual is pilgrimage. A pilgrimage is an undertaking to see and be seen by the deity.

Many Hindus embark on pilgrimages to rivers, temples, mountains, and other sacred sites in India. These are places where gods may have appeared or taken form in the human world. The Ganges River is the holiest river in the Hindu religion. Many Hindus make a pilgrimage to the Ganges to bathe in its waters.

HINDU TEMPLES

The design of the Hindu temple reflects many elements of the Hindu faith. The layout, plan, and building process all incorporate ancient rituals, symbols, and beliefs. While Hindu temples come in many styles and variations, most share certain core ideas, symbolism, and themes. You can explore Hindu temples and their design on these websites.

🔍 Hindu temple design

A Hindu who dies at Varanasi and has his or her ashes spread on the Ganges River is believed to have experienced the best death.

One popular pilgrimage is the Kumbh Mela festival. Every 12 years, nearly 10 million people gather at Allahabad, where the Ganges and Yamuna Rivers meet. They participate in ritual bathing to wash away their sins, spiritual purification rituals, and a ceremony to receive blessings from the deity.

Other pilgrims travel to the city of Varanasi, also known as Benares. It is located on the banks of the Ganges River and is believed to be the home of Lord Shiva. Hindu legend says that here is where Shiva's fiery light broke through the earth to reach the heavens.

YOGA

Have you ever done downward facing dog or triangle pose? Studies show that more than 20 million people in the United States practice yoga. It's a very popular form of exercise!

Yoga has spiritual roots in Hinduism. The word yoga comes from the Sanskrit word yug, meaning "to unite." Hindu texts talk about yoga as a practice to control the senses and the mind. Ideas about yoga can be found in the Upanishads and in the ancient Bhagavad Gita text.

A more detailed account of yoga appears in the Yoga Sutras, a text that was created around the second century BCE. The Yoga Sutras include a set of techniques to achieve mental calmness and concentration, which are necessary for greater insight. According to the Yoga Sutras, the practice of yoga protects against ignorance, egocentric views, and emotional extremes. It also helps followers avoid the poisons of greed, anger, and delusion.

The practice of yoga recognizes that the body and mind influence each other. A person's thoughts and feelings can affect his or her physical well-being, while posture and physical control can promote mental alertness.

By combining mental and physical aspects, yoga allows both the body and mind to calm and become more sharply focused. Once this occurs, inner insight may emerge.

FESTIVALS

Hindus celebrate several religious festivals throughout the year. Festivals are based on the Hindu calendar and are often related to seasonal changes. The main Hindu festivals are Holi, Dusserah, and Diwali.

Holi began as a fertility festival and it celebrates the New Year in March and the return of spring. Dusserah occurs between late September and mid-October. This is a nine-day festival that celebrates the victory of good over evil.

[One of the most popular Hindu festivals is Diwali, the Festival of Lights.]

Diwali is a five-day celebration that includes food, fireworks, colored sand, and special candles and lamps. It celebrates the victory of good over evil, light over darkness, and knowledge over ignorance. Usually celebrated in the fall, Diwali began as a harvest festival to mark the last harvest of the year and the beginning of the new agricultural year. The lights of Diwali symbolize the inner light that protects people from spiritual darkness.

ORDER OF SOCIETY

An important idea in classical Hinduism is that the order and structure of the universe includes human society. A person's dharma depends on their class, or varna. It also depends on their stage of life, or ashrama.

DIWALI TODAY

Today, Hindus celebrate Diwali with family gatherings, clay lamps, fireworks, bonfires, and sweet treats. Diwali has become a national festival, celebrated by most people of India, regardless of their religion. During Diwali, people decorate their home with clay lamps, or diyas. They create patterns called rangoli on the floor with colored powder or sand. On the third day of the festival, families gather for prayers to the Goddess Lakshmi and for feasts and fireworks.

FACTS ON FAITH

Holi is celebrated with bonfires and lots of color. Dusserrah is celebrated with music, dancing, and re-enactments.

Indian society has been classified into four main groups since ancient times. In the *Rig Veda* you can read a hymn that tells of the body of a human sacrificed and divided to create the four main varnas: Brahmin, Kshatriya, Vaishya, and Shudra.

The Brahmins are intellectuals and priests who perform religious rituals. The Kshatriya are the nobles or warriors. The Vaishyas are members of the merchant class who produce, farm, and trade, while the Shudras are servants. Under the varna system, each varna is essential to the right ordering of the world. Each depends on the others.

> Today, Western ideas of equality, new roles, and nontraditional careers are challenging the traditional ideas of varna. Can you think of other times in history when contemporary life challenged the ideas of religion?

People in the first three varnas are said to be twice-born because they have been born a second time through a sacred-thread ritual. This ritual, called upanayana, marks their acceptance of responsibility as a Hindu. The ritual is usually performed when a male child turns eight years old.

Men who are twice-born go through four stages of life, or ashramas. In the first stage, students are expected to study the Vedas under instruction from a teacher or a guru. In the second stage, a man is expected to marry, have children, and support family and society.

In the third stage, which traditionally begins with the birth of a grandchild, people retire from active work.

They spend their time reflecting on life and advising others. In the final stage of life, which not all Hindus reach, the person gives up on the world and becomes a wandering ascetic.

In traditional Hinduism, women may be classified by varna, but they pass through their own three stages of life. The first stage is as a child protected by her father, then she is a married woman protected by her husband. In the final stage, a woman is a widow protected by her eldest son. These stages of life reflect the traditional Hindu view of women as being more delicate than men and requiring protection.

> In modern times, however, many Hindus are re-examining and changing their ideas about the roles of women.

Hinduism's followers across the world are united in many common beliefs, practices, and traditions. At the same time, Hinduism can be expressed in different ways, each with its own unique traditions. Other, related religions have arisen from these differences, including another of the world's main religions—Buddhism.

SACRIFICE

Historically, sacrifice has been an important part of Hinduism. In Hinduism, sacrifice is an offering to the gods, generally food or drink. Fire is also an important part of sacrifice. Followers believe that ritual sacrifice provides a connection to the deity and also establishes the right order of the world. By making a sacrifice, followers might be protected from evil forces and enjoy abundant crops, good weather, health, and happiness.

KEY QUESTIONS

- How can Hinduism be both monotheistic and polytheistic?

- The concept of samsara, which is the cycle of birth, death, and rebirth, recurs in many contemporary stories. Why do you think humans are attracted to this idea?

- What effect does the concept of varnas, or classes, have on the way people live their lives? Is this a good thing, bad thing, or both? Why?

INTERVIEW A PERSON OF THE HINDU FAITH

One of the best ways to understand a different religion or faith is to talk with a person who is a member of that faith. In this activity, you will discuss the Hindu faith with a person who practices it.

Ideas for Supplies ▼

- pencil and paper
- digital voice recorder (optional)

- **Identify a person who practices Hinduism that you can interview.** He or she might be a classmate, a member of your community, or a coworker of your parents. You can also contact local Hindu temples to ask if someone is willing to be interviewed. Schedule a time to meet or talk over the phone.

- **Before the interview, spend some time thinking of questions about Hinduism.** What would you like to learn more about? What interests you about the religion? Using these ideas, prepare a list of questions for the interview.

- **Conduct the interview at the scheduled time.** Some of the person's answers may spark new questions that you may want to ask. Takes notes and record the person's answers.

- **After the interview, think about what you learned and consider the following questions.**

  1. What have you learned about Hinduism that you did not know previously?

  2. What was the most surprising thing you learned about Hinduism?

  3. How does Hinduism compare to your religion? If you do not practice a religion, think about how it compares to aspects of your life. What similarities are there? What are the differences?

To investigate more, think about an aspect of Hinduism that you want to learn more about. Research it in greater depth and compare what you learn to what you already know. How does this new information change the way you view Hinduism? How does it expand your understanding of this faith?

As you read each chapter in this book and develop an understanding of each religion, interview a member of that faith and ask similar questions.

VOCAB LAB

Write down what you think each word means: **reincarnation**, **transcendent**, **Shiva Nataraja**, **shruti**, **mantras**, **varnas**, **pilgrimage**, **Brahmins**, and **Shakti**.

Compare your definitions with those of your friends or classmates. Did you all come up with the same meanings? Turn to the text and glossary if you need help.

I DIDN'T REALIZE THAT DIWALI IS DEDICATED TO LAKSHMI, TOO!

Ideas for Supplies ▼

- computer with Internet access
- comfortable clothing
- exercise mat

I FEEL A LITTLE CALMER ALREADY...

PRACTICE YOGA

Yoga is an important part of Hinduism, allowing Hindus to clear and silence the mind. In this activity, you will practice several yoga poses.

- **Explore yoga poses with these videos for beginning yoga students.**

🔍 Yoga poses for beginners, where to start? · Foundations of Yoga

- **Practice the different yoga moves with the instructor.** Concentrate on using the yoga poses to still your mind. If you find yourself distracted, simply return your focus to your body and its movement.

- **As you practice the yoga moves, experiment with turning off the volume and performing the moves in silence.** You can also add soothing background music of your choice. What do you prefer: silence, music, or the instructor's voice?

> To investigate more, use the yoga positions that you have learned to create your own yoga routine. Do you find yoga to be better for your body or your mind?

Chapter 2
Judaism

What are the major tenants of Judaism?

Followers of Judaism believe in one true God. They also believe in a covenant between Jews and God.

Founded more than 3,500 years ago in the Middle East, Judaism is one of the oldest surviving religions. It evolved from the beliefs of the people of Canaan, an area of the eastern Mediterranean that today includes most of modern Israel, Jordan, and Syria.

With approximately 14 million followers worldwide, Judaism is the smallest of the major religions. Today, most Jewish people live in either the United States (41 percent) or Israel (41 percent). The remaining live primarily in Canada, France, the United Kingdom, Germany, Russia, and Argentina.

One of the central tenets of Judaism is the belief in a single universal and eternal God who created the world and everything in it. Another pillar of Judaism is the covenant, or promise, between God and the Jewish people.

> Followers of Judaism believe that God has entered into a special relationship with the Jewish people, making them the Chosen People. They believe God has appointed them to set an example of holiness and a standard of ethics for the world.

ABRAHAM AND THE FIRST COVENANT

Judaism traces its beginnings back to the first covenant that God made with a shepherd named Abram, who was later renamed Abraham.

According to Jewish texts, Abram was a shepherd from the city of Ur in Mesopotamia, which is modern-day Iraq. The community in which Abram lived was polytheistic, which meant the people worshipped many gods. Although members of Abram's family also worshipped several gods, Abram believed that there was only one true God. Abram's belief and worship of one god was the start of monotheism.

When Abram was an old man, God called on him to leave home and travel to Canaan. This would become the Israelite homeland.

The promise between God and Abraham was the first covenant. Because of his faith and the first covenant with God, Abraham is considered to be one of the patriarchs of the Jewish people.

THE DIASPORA

When the Babylonians defeated the ancient kingdom of Judea and exiled its people, the Jews spread to different lands. They brought Judaism to many corners of the world in the diaspora, or "dispersion." Judaism developed differently in each land, based on the influence of the local people and cultures.

In return for Abram's obedience, God promised to reward him with many descendants who would inherit the land. God promised that as long as Abram and his descendants obeyed Him, God would protect them and give them the land of Canaan. Abram and his wife, Sarai, did as God asked. In honor of their agreement, God changed Abram's name to Abraham and Sarai's to Sarah, which means "father of the people" and "noblewoman," respectively. Abram's people traveled with him and were known as the Israelites.

Abraham had two sons, Ishmael and Isaac. God tested Abraham again by asking him to sacrifice his beloved son Isaac. Abraham trusted God and took Isaac up a mountain to be sacrificed. At the last moment, God stopped Abraham and spared Isaac's life. God chose Isaac to inherit the covenant from his father.

MOSES AND THE SECOND COVENANT

When Canaan fell into famine, Isaac's son Jacob led the Israelite people to Egypt. There, the Israelites were enslaved by the Egyptians for several generations. Around 1300 BCE, God chose Moses to lead the Israelites out of Egypt and slavery to return to Canaan.

Many miracles enabled the escape of Moses and the Israelites. When Moses first asked the Egyptian pharaoh for the Israelites' freedom, the pharaoh refused. But after God struck the Egyptians with 10 plagues, the pharaoh allowed the Israelites to leave.

The second covenant between God and Moses renewed God's promise to the Jewish people to protect them as long as they were faithful.

When the pharaoh changed his mind and sent his army to stop them, God helped the Israelites again by parting the waters of the Red Sea and allowing them to pass through unharmed. Then the waters poured back into place and drowned the Egyptian soldiers.

Moses led the Israelites through the desert for almost three months. While Moses was camping by Mount Sinai, God appeared to him high on the mountain. God made the second covenant with the Israelites, one that renewed his promise to Abraham.

> God promised the Israelites that they would be his chosen people if they obeyed his laws. These laws were given to Moses on two stone tablets. They outlined the basic rules for the Israelites to follow in daily life.

BELIEF IN ONE GOD

In Judaism, God is transcendent and the creator of the world. Unlike the gods of polytheistic religions, which are shown in various animal and human forms, the Jewish God is formless and invisible, beyond the ability of humans to understand or even describe. The Jewish people also believe God is just and merciful.

The Ten Commandments have formed the basis of moral behavior for more than 3,000 years. The majority of the world's people, including those who follow Judaism and Christianity, follow these commandments.

THE TEN COMMANDMENTS

On Mount Sinai, God gave Moses the Torah, which means "law." It contains 613 commandments, the rules God said they should live by, which cover every part of life, including law, family, personal hygiene, and diet.

The most famous of these commandments are called the Ten Commandments. They summarize the most fundamental rules of the Israelites' covenant with God and read as follows.

1. I am the Lord thy God.

2. Thou shalt have no other gods before me.

3. Thou shalt not take the name of the Lord thy God in vain.

4. Remember the Sabbath day and keep it holy.

5. Honour thy father and thy mother.

6. Thou shalt not commit murder.

7. Thou shalt not commit adultery.

8. Thou shalt not steal.

9. Thou shalt not bear false witness against thy neighbour.

10. Thou shalt not covet anything that is thy neighbour's.

Through the years, the commandments have been interpreted in different ways. But many laws that pertain to observing the Sabbath, festivals, dietary restrictions, and treatment of other human beings are still followed by the Jewish people.

SACRED TEXTS

The followers of Judaism believe that while Moses was on Mount Sinai he received the Torah from God. The Torah became the most important sacred text of Judaism. Commandments written in the Torah show how God wants the Jewish people to live.

The Torah is made of five books—Genesis, Exodus, Leviticus, Numbers, and Deuteronomy. Ritual laws, rules of hygiene, and moral codes are included in its commandments. As God's Chosen People, Jews are called to live by these laws because they are part of the covenant relationship with God.

> The Torah is part of the Tanakh. The Tanakh also contains the 21 books of the prophets and 13 books of writings.

The written Torah does not give much explanation or instruction on how to apply its laws to specific situations. But followers of Judaism believe that God taught Moses how to apply the laws. Known as the Oral Law, these teachings were passed down orally from generation to generation of Israelites. The Oral Law contained information that the Israelites needed to fully follow the Torah's written commandments.

Around the second century CE, Jewish rabbis began to write down the teachings of the Oral Law. Many of the rabbis' writings form a set of books called the Talmud. Collected from the writings of thousands of rabbis during hundreds of years, the Talmud contains the Mishnah and the Gemara.

FACTS ON FAITH

The people who appear in religious stories might not have been historically real people, but instead are figures that followers of the religion believe in and use to explain different things.

The Torah is written in Hebrew, the language of the ancient Israelites. It is traditionally written with no vowels—only consonants.

Some followers of Judaism believe that the Messiah will be a human ruler. Some believe there will be what's called a Messianic Age, without crime, war, and poverty.

The text of the Mishnah is the written version of the Oral Law. The Gemara interprets and discusses the law. The Talmud is important because it analyzes and interprets Jewish laws.

> For example, the Torah prohibited working on the Sabbath, but it did not explain what was considered to be "work." The Talmud gives specific examples of work that is forbidden on the Sabbath, such as building, cooking, and writing.

THE MESSIAH

King David, a descendant of Abraham, ruled over the kingdom of Israel from around 1005 to 965 BCE. According to Jewish history, God also established a covenant with King David and promised that his descendants would rule the land forever. But the Babylonians defeated the southern part of Israel, which was called Judea, in 586 BCE. The Babylonians exiled its people and destroyed the Temple of Jerusalem. With this defeat, the rule of kings in Israel ended. Yet the Jewish people hoped that, according to God's promise, one of King David's descendants would once again rule the land as the Messiah, which means "God's anointed one" in Hebrew.

Many Jewish people believe that the coming of the Messiah will bring about the golden Messianic Age. This will mean a return of the Jewish people to Israel.

Most believe that the Messianic Age will be a period of peace on Earth, during which the Messiah will right all wrongs in the world and end all wars. The Messiah will establish God's kingdom on Earth.

Throughout history, there have been a few individuals that some people believed were the Messiah. Christians believe that Jesus of Nazareth was the Messiah, although followers of Judaism do not agree.

> Today, some followers of Judaism wait for the true Messiah, believing that he has not yet appeared in the world.

PRAYER AND WORSHIP

In the Jewish religion, reciting prayers is the most common form of worship. Although some prayer can be individual, group prayer is important in the Jewish faith. Traditionally, prayers were only said in the presence of a group of at least 10 men, which is called a minyan. In more progressive groups, women count toward the minyan, too.

The synagogue has become the center for Jewish worship and study. Many synagogues hold formal services three times a day. They offer lessons in Judaism for children and adults. Many adults study there, using libraries of sacred texts. The synagogue also serves as a social gathering place for the Jewish community.

Inside a synagogue, a rabbi, cantor, or other member of the congregation leads the services. Traditionally, a Jewish worship service needs a minyan in order to occur. A service can vary in content and length. In orthodox synagogues, the services are in ancient Hebrew, with unaccompanied singing and chanting.

HASIDISM

Hasidism is a religious movement that arose in Eastern Europe in the late 1700s. Hasidic Jews are easily recognizable by their black suits, black hats, side-curls, and beards. The women dress modestly and married women wear wigs. Hasidic Jews are strongly Orthodox. They live in separate communities and follow their own customs. Large groups of Hasidic Jews live in Israel and in some places in the United States.

FACTS ON FAITH

A synagogue is sometimes called a "temple" by Reform Jews and a "shul" by Orthodox Jews. The word *shul* comes from the German word *schule*, which means school.

Men and women are often segregated in synagogues and do not sit together. In other synagogues, the service may be conducted partly in English, include instruments, and allow men and women to sit together.

Inside a synagogue, everyone except unmarried women wears a head covering to show respect to God. Jewish men wear a small round cap called a yarmulke. Adult men over the age of 13 may also wear a prayer shawl called a tallit. The fringes on the tallit remind its wearer to follow God's commandments.

THE TORAH SCROLL

Every synagogue has an ark, which is a cabinet to hold the Torah scrolls. Above the ark, an eternal light called a Ner Tamid burns as a symbol of God's presence and the pillar of fire that guided the Jewish people's flight from Egypt. When the rabbi or cantor reads from the Torah, they use a platform and desk called a bimah.

> During the service, the ark is opened and the Torah scroll is carried to the reading desk, where it is unrolled to the reading for the day.

The entire text of the Torah is handwritten by a scribe in Hebrew on a long scroll. The parchment for the scroll comes from a kosher animal, usually a cow. It can take the scribe up to 18 months to prepare a scroll. If the scribe makes a mistake, the entire scroll is ruined. They have to be very careful!

Followers of Judaism believe that the first Torah scroll was written by Moses, who wrote down God's direct words. From that original scroll, many copies have been handwritten by scribes throughout the centuries. Today, there are hundreds of thousands of Torah scrolls all around the world.

The handwritten scroll is rolled around two ornate wooden shafts, each attached to one end of the scroll. Each week, the scroll is read aloud in the synagogue by a rabbi or other trained person. The reading of the Torah scroll takes skill and practice. The words are written without vowels and are sung or chanted using an ancient tune. Through an entire year, the whole scroll is read in sequence.

BRANCHES OF JUDAISM

Because of their migration to different countries, the Jewish people have developed unique sects with different beliefs and practices. Today, the three major branches of Judaism are Orthodox, Reform, and Conservative Judaism. These branches have their own interpretations of the Hebrew texts and observe their faith in different ways.

DIETARY RESTRICTIONS

Kashrut is the section of Jewish laws that deal with which foods Jewish people can eat and how those foods should be prepared and eaten. A common term for this is "kosher," which describes food that meets these standards. One kosher dietary law states that meat cannot be eaten with dairy. Another law permits eating meat from animals that have cloven hooves and chew their cud, such as cattle and sheep. Eating meat from animals that do not meet this criteria, such as the pig, is forbidden. Many Jewish people follow kosher dietary laws all year. There are additional dietary restrictions during the Passover holiday. For example, leavened bread may be fine to eat during the year, but it is not kosher for Passover.

The Jewish day begins at sunset, which means that all Jewish holidays begin the evening before their calendar dates.

FACTS ON FAITH

Traditionally, men and women pray separately in Judaism. This tradition dates back to the time of the Temple of Jerusalem, when it was thought that women distracted men from prayer.

Orthodox Judaism is the most traditional of the three major branches. Orthodox Jews believe that the entire Torah, including the Oral Law, was given to Moses by God at Mount Sinai. This remains the ultimate authority for how to live life, even in modern times. Orthodox Jews observe the traditional practices of daily worship, dietary laws, traditional prayers, regular study of the Torah, and separation of men and women in the synagogue.

[
Orthodox Jews also strictly observe the Sabbath and other religious festivals and holidays.
]

Reform Judaism is a more liberal version of Judaism. In the early 1800s, some Jews in Western Europe and the United States wanted to update Jewish traditions and adapt them to modern life. While followers of Reform Judaism accept the faith's central pillars of God, the Torah, and Israel, they are more liberal in other practices. Women may serve as rabbis and cantors. Reform Jews are generally more accepting of change, welcoming interfaith families and homosexuals into synagogue life.

Conservative Judaism falls between the Orthodox and Reform branches. Conservative Jews value preserving some of Judaism's traditional elements, but also accept some modernization of the faith. The Sabbath and dietary laws are observed but with some modifications. In Conservative synagogues, women may be rabbis.

RITES AND RITUALS

As with many religions, Judaism observes several rites and rituals during a follower's life. As a sign of the covenant between God and Abraham, all male members of his household were circumcised. The brit milah is an important rite where an eight-day-old baby boy is circumcised and given a Hebrew name.

At the age of 13, a boy is considered an adult under traditional Jewish law and is expected to obey all the commandments. The bar mitzvah ceremony marks this rite of passage. Many Reform Jews celebrate a similar ceremony for girls, called a bat mitzvah, which takes place at age 12. After much preparation, the children read from the Torah scroll during the Sabbath morning service. Upon completion of this ceremony, people can lead religious services, count toward a minyan, and enter into contracts.

In the Jewish faith, when a person dies, burial takes place as soon as possible. The deceased person is ritually bathed and dressed in a traditional burial garment, usually a white linen shroud. The shroud symbolizes that everyone is equal in death. It does not have pockets, reminding us that we take nothing with us when we die and that God will judge a person on his or her deeds, not material wealth. The deceased is buried in a simple wooden casket that has no metal parts and then carried to the grave, where a rabbi and mourners recite prayers for the dead. For seven days after a death, family and friends pay respects during a time called shiva. Often, people gather in the home of the deceased and say prayers and share meals.

THE TEMPLE OF JERUSALEM

According to Jewish history, King David made Jerusalem the capital of his kingdom. King David's son, Solomon, built the first temple there as the center of worship. The Temple of Jerusalem held the Ark of the Covenant with the original stone tablets that Moses received from God. Destroyed by the Babylonians, the Temple of Jerusalem was rebuilt by King Herod and destroyed again by the Romans. Only part of the wall built around Herod's temple remains. Known as the Western Wall or the Wailing Wall, it has become the most sacred place in the Jewish world.

CHANT THE PASSOVER FOUR QUESTIONS

THE SABBATH AND HOLIDAYS

Followers of Judaism celebrate the Sabbath. This day of rest begins on Friday night and ends on Saturday night. Jews light candles to symbolize the end of God's creation of the world, when his work was completed.

Jewish holidays such as Passover, Shavuot, and Sukkoth are related to Israel's history and agriculture. Rosh Hashanah and Yom Kippur are times for reflection, repentance, and prayers of forgiveness. Hanukkah and Purim celebrate the saving of the Jewish people.

Rosh Hashanah is the celebration of the Jewish New Year. It is the time when Jews believe God decides what will happen in the year ahead. It also the time for God's judgment, when God balances a follower's good vs. bad deeds and decides their fate.

Yom Kippur, known as the Day of Atonement, is a sacred and solemn holiday. Traditionally, followers believe that God makes the final decision on who will live, die, succeed, or fail during the following year. Some people observe this day with fasting and worship, where they confess sins and ask for God's forgiveness.

Hanukkah is a celebration of the miracle of the oil. According to Jewish history, a group of Jews recaptured Jerusalem from Syrians around 164 BCE. When they came to rededicate the temple, they only had enough oil to light the menorah for one day, but the light burned for eight days.

To celebrate this event, Jews light candles on a special nine-branched menorah for eight days. They pray, eat food fried in oil, and exchange gifts.

Passover is one of the most important Jewish festivals. This is when the Jewish people remember the flight of the Israelites from Egypt and God's sparing of the Israelites' oldest sons. To celebrate Passover, Jewish families prepare a ritual meal for friends and family called a seder.

KEY QUESTIONS

- **Why is the concept of a covenant between God and the Hebrew people a central belief in Judaism? How does it influence Judaism's practices?**

- **Jews believe that God gave Moses a set of commandments or rules for life. What effect do the commandments have on the way people live their lives? Is this a good thing, bad thing, or both? Why?**

- **Who is the Messiah in Judaism and what is the role of the Messiah? How does this belief differ from other faiths?**

THE HOLOCAUST

Throughout history, the Jewish people have faced persecution. Often living as a minority, they have been discriminated against and harmed by others. One of the most horrific examples of this persecution was the Holocaust. In 1933, Adolf Hitler became the chancellor of Germany. He believed that the Jews were an inferior race of people. During World War II (1939–1945), Hitler's German army occupied most of Europe. Hitler's soldiers gathered the Jews and sent them to concentration camps, where they were systematically murdered. It is estimated that 6 million Jews and up to 13 million people in all were killed during the Holocaust. The Holocaust is also known as the Shoah, which means "catastrophe" in Hebrew.

YIKES, I'M GLAD OUR DAD JUST TAKES US CAMPING.

SACRED TEXT: THE STORY OF ABRAHAM AND ISAAC

Most religions have sacred texts. Sacred texts are known as scripture, holy writ, or holy books. They contain the writing that followers believe to be central to their religious traditions. Many religions believe that their sacred texts are revealed or inspired by a deity.

Sacred texts often include religious stories that have meaning for a faith's followers. In this activity, you will learn the story of Abraham and Isaac from the Jewish Bible.

* **Read the story of Abraham and Isaac here.**

🔍 Jewish bible Abraham Isaac

* **After reading this sacred story, consider the following questions.**

  1. What message did this sacred story send to followers of Judaism in ancient times?

  2. Does this story still have meaning to Jews living in today's world? Why or why not?

  3. How can a text written thousands of years ago help followers live their lives today?

  4. Discuss your answers with your classmates. How are your answers similar? How are they different?

To investigate more, select another story from a sacred Jewish text. You can use another story at chabad.org or another source. How does this story compare to the one you have already read? What message did it have for ancient Jews? Is its message still relevant today? Does the language in these stories sound different than language we use in stories today? How?

FINDING FACTS IN SACRED TEXT

In addition to providing information about faith, sacred texts can be used to shed light on what life was like in ancient times. Archaeologists use the Bible along with artifacts and other writings to learn more about how people lived in the Near East thousands of years ago. Archaeology may unearth objects and artifacts, but the stories in sacred texts help put these items into context and show how and why they were used.

In this activity, you will read some passages from the Jewish Torah and investigate some of the historical facts you can learn.

- **In the Torah, read Deuteronomy 28.** If you do not have access to a Jewish Bible, you can use one online at this website. Select the book Deuteronomy and chapter 28.

$\bigcirc$ online Jewish Bible

- **What clues do you find in the text about how ancient Jews lived?** Consider the following questions.

  - What are some of the foods they ate?

  - What kinds of animals did they have?

  - What kinds of objects did they use in daily life?

  - What types of illnesses did they experience?

  - What other facts did you learn about Jewish life in ancient times? How do these facts support the work of archaeologists?

To investigate more, select another chapter from the Torah. What new facts did you learn about historical life for the Jewish people? Why is it important to study religious texts for meaning beyond what a people believes in?

VOCAB LAB

Write down what you think each word means: **covenant, plague, Torah, Messianic Age, minyan, synagogue, orthodox,** and **Holocaust**.

Compare your definitions with those of your friends or classmates. Did you all come up with the same meanings? Turn to the text and glossary if you need help.

Ideas for Supplies ▼

- packet of yeast (available in the grocery store)
- small, clean, clear, plastic bottle
- sugar
- warm water
- small balloon

To investigate more, do some research on yeast. What happens when the yeast interacts with sugar? What is being released into the balloon? What happens in bread dough to cause it to rise? Repeat this project using cold water and a cold place. What happens? Are your results the same or different?

UNLEAVENED BREAD FOR PASSOVER

Every year, followers of Judaism celebrate Passover in remembrance of the Jewish people's flight from slavery in ancient Egypt more than 3,000 years ago. In the story of the Exodus, God helped Moses and the Israelites escape from Egypt by sending 10 plagues upon the Egyptians.

After the 10th plague, the Egyptian pharaoh freed the Israelites. They left in such a hurry that they did not have time to wait for their bread dough to rise.

During the eight days of Passover, Jewish people eat unleavened bread in remembrance of the Israelites' flight out of Egypt. Yeast is the ingredient in bread dough that makes it rise. Watch what yeast does to the balloon.

- **Blow up the balloon and let it deflate a few times to stretch it out.**
- **Pour about one inch of warm water into the bottle.**
- **Add all of the yeast in the package and gently swirl the bottle for a few seconds.**
- **Add a teaspoon of sugar and swirl it around some more to mix thoroughly.**
- **Seal the balloon over the neck of the bottle.**
- **Let the bottle sit in a warm place for about 20 minutes.** What happens to the balloon?

Chapter 3
Buddhism

What do people who follow Buddhism believe? What are their values?

 Buddhists believe they can reach enlightenment through compassion for all living things.

Buddhism originated in India more than 2,500 years ago. Today, Buddhism has spread to many countries around the world and has nearly 500 million followers. The word *Buddhism* comes from the word *budh*, which means "to awaken."

Although it is considered a religion, Buddhism is viewed by many people to be more of a philosophy or a way of life. Buddhism's followers focus on personal spiritual development. Following the path and example set by the founder of Buddhism, Buddhist followers strive to achieve a deeper insight into the true nature of life.

The universal goal of Buddhism is to achieve a state of enlightenment and a freedom from suffering, which come about through acts of compassion for all living things. Today, Buddhism is considered to be the fourth-largest religion, behind Christianity, Islam, and Hinduism.

ORIGINS OF BUDDHISM

Buddhism's spiritual traditions can be traced back to Siddhartha Gautama, who was known by his followers as the Buddha, or the Awakened One. According to Buddhist history, Siddhartha Gautama was born around 563 BCE into a royal family. He lived in the town of Lumbini in northeast India, in an area that is present-day Nepal. Gautama was well-educated and lived a privileged life in his father's palace, with many comforts. As a young man, he married a princess and had a son.

In his early thirties, Gautama became restless and curious about life outside his palace enclosure, which he had never left. Can you imagine spending your life in one place and never visiting a neighboring town? Would you be restless?

FACTS ON FAITH

Buddha taught that the root of all suffering is desire, which comes in three forms—greed, ignorance, and hatred.

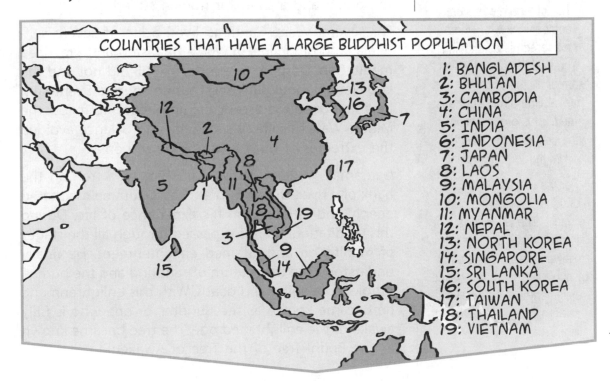

COUNTRIES THAT HAVE A LARGE BUDDHIST POPULATION

1: BANGLADESH
2: BHUTAN
3: CAMBODIA
4: CHINA
5: INDIA
6: INDONESIA
7: JAPAN
8: LAOS
9: MALAYSIA
10: MONGOLIA
11: MYANMAR
12: NEPAL
13: NORTH KOREA
14: SINGAPORE
15: SRI LANKA
16: SOUTH KOREA
17: TAIWAN
18: THAILAND
19: VIETNAM

When Gautama ventured outside the royal grounds for the first time, he saw three things that he had never before seen: a sick man, an old man, and a corpse. These sights greatly upset Gautama. This was his first exposure to the extent of human suffering.

[He learned that sickness, old age, and death were parts of human life that could not be escaped.]

In another trip outside the palace walls, Gautama saw a fourth sight: a wandering ascetic, or shramana. He took this as a sign that he should leave his pampered life, follow the ascetic's example, and live as a wandering holy man. Gautama gave up his princely title and became a monk. He left on a religious quest to find the origin and answer for human suffering.

For several years, Gautama lived a life of severe self-denial and discipline, in which he fasted and practiced meditation. Despite his efforts, he still did not find the knowledge about suffering that he sought. Eventually, he abandoned the ascetic life and began to follow the Middle Way. This life of simplicity and balance avoided the extremes of both luxury and self-denial.

Gautama's wanderings brought him to a tree on the bank of a river. Under its branches, Gautama meditated deeply and reflected on his experience of life. During this meditation, Gautama passed through all the stages of meditation and attained enlightenment. He finally understood the true nature of suffering and the human problems of aging and death. With this enlightenment, he became known as the Buddha, or one who is fully awake or the enlightened one. The tree became known as the Bodhi Tree or the Tree of Awakening.

CYCLE OF REBIRTH

In India, where Buddha lived, many people believed in the Hindu idea of samsara. They believed that a person's soul was caught in an eternal cycle of birth and rebirth. In the Hindu traditions, religious practices such as worship and ritual were key components of escaping this cycle.

Buddha accepted the idea of the cycle of rebirth but suggested a different way to break the cycle. Instead of religious worship and rituals, Buddha taught that people should change their ways of life. Instead of blindly following sacred texts, Buddha suggested that his teachings should be a starting point that followers could use for personal meditation and understanding.

The main obstacle to escaping the cycle of rebirth was human suffering, which was caused by desires and attachments that could never be satisfied. Buddha explained how suffering could be overcome in the Four Noble Truths.

FACTS ON FAITH

Upon Buddha's death, he reached his final nirvana and escaped the suffering of rebirth. Following his instructions, several of his followers cremated his body. They spread Buddha's ashes as relics in mounds called stupas. Over time, these stupas have become important Buddhist pilgrimage sites.

THE FOUR NOBLE TRUTHS

BUDDHA'S SON

According to Buddhist texts, after Buddha left his palace on his search for enlightenment, his son, Rahula, was raised by his mother and grandfather. When Rahula was about seven years old, Buddha returned to his hometown of Kapilavastu. Rahula's mother took him to listen to Buddha's sermon and told her son to ask his father for his inheritance. Buddha decided to take him as a disciple and Rahula became an eager and attentive student.

In his first sermon, Buddha described the Four Noble Truths, which have become the central teachings of Buddhism. They focus on what Buddha learned about suffering through his enlightenment and how to end it. These are the Four Noble Truths.

1. **Dukkha**, the truth of suffering
2. **Samudaya**, the truth of the origin of suffering
3. **Nirodha**, the truth of the end of suffering
4. **Magga**, the truth of the path to the end of suffering

The Four Noble Truths say that suffering exists and something causes it, but suffering can end and there is a way to bring about its end.

Dukkha affirms that all life involves suffering. Life is not perfect—it is fragile and messy. Suffering can be physical or mental. It can involve intense pain or feelings of dissatisfaction. Suffering occurs when a loved one dies or when a person is stuck in an unpleasant situation, such as a long wait at the doctor's office. Can you think of times when you have suffered?

> The Second Noble Truth teaches samudaya, that the cause of suffering is desire and the craving for things to be a certain way.

The Second Noble Truth, samudaya, attempts to find the cause of suffering. According to Buddha, the search for happiness often leads people in the wrong direction. People crave things such as pleasure, wealth, power, and material possessions, believing that these things can bring happiness. Do you ever feel as though your life would be perfect if you could just buy the next-generation iPod? But would it really be perfect?

Buddha taught that instead of bringing happiness, these cravings only bring suffering and more unhappiness. Clinging to certain views, ideas, rules, and observances is also a form of craving. He warned that clinging to old beliefs causes suffering. In this way, Buddhism differs from other religions, which encourage followers to have faith in doctrines and certain rituals.

Buddha's Third Noble Truth, nirodha, says that a person can end suffering by removing himself from craving and desire. Buddha taught that if craving stopped, suffering would also stop. By ending suffering, an individual can achieve nirvana.

The Fourth Noble Truth, magga, sets out the path for followers to end suffering. This path is called the Noble Eightfold Path.

FACTS ON FAITH

The Mahabodhi Temple at the site of Buddha's enlightenment is now a pilgrimage site.

BUDDHIST MONKS

Many of Buddha's followers were monks. At first, these men were wandering teachers like Buddha himself. Later, groups of monks settled in monastic communities. Here, they followed steps designed to benefit their own spiritual development as well as help people in the community.

Today, monastic life remains an important part of Buddhism, especially in the countries of Sri Lanka and Thailand, which follow the Theravada Buddhist tradition. These Buddhist monks take their vows for a short period. Their vows help them work on personal enlightenment and focus on developing compassion for others.

FACTS ON FAITH

Buddha's teaching is called the Middle Way. It calls on Buddhist followers to choose a middle way of life that balances the extremes of luxury and austerity.

THE NOBLE EIGHTFOLD PATH

Buddhism's way to end suffering is described as a path with eight steps. The path's steps do not need to be taken in any specific order. The Noble Eightfold Path is more like a set of eight principles that allows Buddhists to conquer cravings and achieve happiness.

- **Right Understanding:** accepting and practicing Buddhist teachings

- **Right Thought:** being committed to developing the right attitudes

- **Right Speech:** speaking truthfully and avoiding gossip

- **Right Action:** behaving peacefully and not stealing, killing, or overindulging

- **Right Livelihood:** making a living in a way that causes no harm to others, such as killing animals or selling alcohol

- **Right Effort:** encouraging a positive state of mind

- **Right Mindfulness:** being aware of the body and the mind

- **Right Concentration:** developing mental focus

The Noble Eightfold Path suggests a way of life that reduces suffering. The path can be grouped into three basic themes: wisdom (right understanding and thought), virtue (right speech, action, and livelihood), and concentration or meditation (effort, mindfulness, and concentration). Each individual can concentrate on different parts of the path based on their specific circumstances.

SPREAD OF BUDDHISM

Buddhism quickly spread through India and northward into China. As it spread, different traditions emerged. The two largest traditions are Theravada Buddhism and Mahayana Buddhism.

Theravada Buddhism is closest to Buddha's original teachings and is most popular in Sri Lanka, Cambodia, Thailand, Laos, and Burma. Mahayana Buddhism is mainly practiced in Tibet, China, Taiwan, Japan, Korea, and Mongolia. Mahayana Buddhism uses rich symbols and images of the Buddha. It also has religious leaders, known as bodhisattvas, who have achieved enlightenment but have chosen to be reborn to help others on the path.

Later divisions led to the branch called Zen Buddhism, which strives to clear the mind in order to allow spontaneous enlightenment without the use of ritual scriptures. Tibetan Buddhism is known for its colorful temples, images, and rituals.

> Despite their differences, all Buddhist traditions aim to help followers on a path of enlightenment.

THE WHEEL OF LIFE

One of the main tenets of Buddha's teaching is the idea that everything is interconnected. Everything happens because something caused it or is connected to it. The goal of Buddhism is to create conditions that cause sadness and suffering to be replaced with happiness and contentment. What makes you unhappy? Does anything in your life cause you sadness?

THE EMPEROR ASOKA

The son of the Mauryan emperor, Asoka was born in India in 304 BCE. After he took the throne in 268 BCE, Asoka embarked on a campaign to extend his rule. He fought to build an empire that included most of India. After one extremely bloody battle, the sight of the dead and grieving caused Asoka to swear he would never fight a battle again. He turned to Buddhism for answers and became a passionate follower. After his conversion, Asoka promoted Buddhist principles throughout his empire. He banned animal sacrifices and provided welfare to the needy. He also sent missionaries to promote Buddhism in foreign lands. Have you ever quit a hurtful habit after a bad experience? Were you happier afterward?

If you practice Buddhism, you might look at the causes for your unhappiness. Then you can consider changes that lead you to follow a different, happier path.

The Wheel of Life shows a visual form of the cycle of life, death, rebirth, and suffering that Buddhists seek to escape through enlightenment. The circular wheel represents the endless cycle of existence and suffering. In the center of the wheel, a rooster, snake, and a pig represent the three poisons of greed, hatred, and ignorance. The ring around the center represents karma.

Pictures show figures ascending or descending into the six realms of existence: gods, demi-gods, humans animals, hungry ghosts, and hell-beings. Figures ascend to higher realms because of virtuous actions. Other figures descend into lower realms because of evil or ignorant actions. Twelve links on the wheel's outer rim speak to the interconnectedness that is key to Buddhist teachings.

The wheel is held by a demon called Yama, the Lord of Death. Yama symbolizes the inevitability of death, rebirth, and the impermanence of the universe. Outside the wheel, Buddha points the way to liberation, which gives hope.

The pictures on the Wheel of Life remind followers that everyone is responsible for his or her fate. This is because, according to karma, causes and their effects are the results of one's actions.

> The Wheel of Life represents the endless cycle of death and rebirth in which you are trapped unless you follow the Middle Way to enlightenment.

ORIGIN OF THE UNIVERSE

Buddhism does not have a creator god to explain the origin of the universe. Instead, Buddhists believe in interconnectedness, the idea that everything depends on everything else. Events in the present are caused by past events. Present events become the cause of future events. In Buddhism, the creation of the universe happened naturally without intervention from a deity.

In one tale told by Buddha, the world had been destroyed and its inhabitants were reborn into a new universe as luminescent spirits, floating happily without form, name, or gender. Eventually, the earth appeared and the spirits tasted and enjoyed it. Greed caused their bodies to become solid and rough, and to develop into male and female. As the sun and moon emerged, they lost their luminescence. As the beings developed more wicked habits, they caused the earth and themselves to become less pleasant. In this way, the cravings of desire, greed, and attachment caused suffering for the people and the world. The physical world came into being because of this suffering.

PERSONAL DEVELOPMENT

In many religions, the core beliefs are based on the authority of a particular leader, a class of priests, or sacred texts. Followers accept these beliefs without question. Buddhism, however, values questioning and debate. The Buddhist tradition looks to the teachings of Buddha and other religious teachers, but they are seen as starting points.

CAUSE AND EFFECT

Buddha accepted the Hindu idea of samsara, which states that there is a cycle of rebirth and that the outcomes of each life are dependent on your actions in previous lives. Yet Buddhist teaching centers on the idea that nothing is permanent. Followers don't believe that humans have eternal souls, as in the Hindu tradition. Therefore, the Buddha did not believe in the Hindu tradition of sacrifice. Instead of sacrificing animals, Buddhism encourages followers to become self-giving to others, and to work on their own personal spiritual development.

FACTS ON FAITH

During the last 50 years, meditation has grown in popularity in Western cultures. Many people who are not Buddhists practice Buddhist meditation as a way to develop concentration and reduce stress. People also use meditation to cope with chronic pain and depression.

SACRED BUDDHIST TEXTS

The Pali Canon contains stories that teach the concepts of Buddhism. You can read translations of these stories for yourself and decide whether or not they apply to your own life.

PS

🔍 Buddhist Pali Canon translation

> Buddha taught that his followers should not accept his teachings on trust, but should test his suggestions and use their own personal experiences to shape their beliefs.

Buddhist wisdom occurs in three stages—from teachers or sacred texts, personal reflection and thought, and spiritual practice. Spiritual practice often includes meditation and using Buddhist teachings in daily life. In this way, Buddhist followers are encouraged to apply Buddha's teachings to their own lives. Buddhists believe that spiritual beliefs should be based on personal experience rather than simply accepting what another person has to say.

SACRED TEXTS

For more than four centuries after the Buddha's death, his followers passed down his teachings by word of mouth. Around the first century BCE, the Buddha's teachings were written down in Sri Lanka in a language called Pali. These texts, called the Pali Canon, are the sacred texts of the Theravada Buddhist tradition.

The Pali Canon is divided into three sections. The Vinaya Pitaka contains teachings on a monk's life. The Sutta Pitaka is a collection of the Buddha's sayings and stories about events in his life. The Abhidhamma Pitaka is a philosophical analysis of the Buddha's teachings.

The Mahayana Sutras, which are the sacred texts of the Mahayana Buddhist tradition, followed the Pali Canon. These are commentaries that interpreted Buddha's teaching.

MEDITATION

In Buddhism, the practice of meditation involves both the body and the mind. Have you ever focused so well on something that you find yourself sitting up straighter and blocking out the rest of the world? Meditation is a way to take control of your mind so it becomes more peaceful and focused.

Some people say that the goal of meditation is to still the mind. You can turn your awareness away from the outside world and focus on inner thoughts, feelings, and perceptions through meditation. Oddly enough, when your mind is quiet and focused you actually become more aware of everything around you.

> Meditation can be practiced in a group, which reminds a person that they are part of a larger Buddhist community and part of a larger community of humans. Meditation can also be practiced individually.

The classical meditation position is the lotus position. To try it, sit cross-legged on the floor with your left foot on top of your right thigh and your right foot on top of your left thigh.

You can also simply sit on the floor in a kneeling or cross-legged position or meditate in a chair. Any meditation position should allow the body to be relaxed, stable, and alert, so your mind can focus.

THE FIVE PRECEPTS

Even though there are several branches of Buddhism, all Buddhists follow a set of guidelines for daily life called the Five Precepts.

1. Do not kill or harm living things.

2. Do not steal.

3. Do not misuse sex.

4. Do not speak unkindly or tell lies.

5. Do not abuse drugs or drink alcohol.

These precepts are considered recommendations, not commandments. Followers are expected to use their own judgment in applying the Five Precepts to their lives.

BUDDHIST CHANTING

Chanting is a part of many Buddhist worship practices. At this website, you can listen to several different examples and styles of Buddhist chants and mantras.

🔍 Buddhist chanting audio

I SAY MY MANTRA, "OM," WHILE I MEDITATE TO HELP ME FOCUS. BUT YOU CAN MAKE UP YOUR OWN IF YOU WANT.

OKAY, I'LL TRY!

OMMMM....

UMMMM....

BUDDHIST SHRINES

Upon the Buddha's death, he reached his final nirvana and escaped the suffering of rebirth. According to his instructions, Buddha's followers cremated his body after his death. They placed his ashes in a series of stupas, or funerary mounds. These stupas served as important pilgrimage sites for worship and meditation.

In its basic form, the Buddhist stupa had a large central mound surrounded by a railing. It was topped by a square structure with a central post that held a series of parasols. As the stupa evolved, people decorated it with representations of the Buddha, events from his life, or stories from Buddhist texts. Buddhist followers make offerings at these shrines with flowers, candles, incense, and similar items. In China, Korea, and Japan, the stupa evolved into large pagoda shrines.

WORSHIP

Buddhism can be practiced at home or at a temple. At home, followers will set up a shrine in a separate room or part of a room. The shrine often includes a statue of Buddha, candles, and an incense burner. Followers may worship by chanting while sitting barefoot on the floor in front of the shrine or an image of Buddha.

Buddhists may utter a mantra as they worship. A mantra is a word, syllable, phrase, or short prayer that is spoken once or repeated over and over. It can be said aloud or in one's mind. The mantra is believed to have a profound spiritual effect on the worshipper.

> Some worshippers use prayer beads to mark the number of repetitions of a mantra. Prayer wheels and prayer flags might be used to display mantras.

Buddhist followers also worship in temples. Some of the most recognizable temples are the ornate Buddhist pagodas of China and Japan. No matter what form they take, Buddhist temples use a design that symbolizes the five elements of fire, air, earth, water, and wisdom. The temple's square base represents Earth, while the pinnacle at its top symbolizes wisdom. In addition, every Buddhist temple contains an image of Buddha.

In a temple, worshippers may sit on the floor barefoot, face an image of Buddha, and chant a mantra. They listen to monks chanting from religious texts. Buddhists can also participate in prayers and chanting with other worshippers.

RITUALS

Most Buddhist rituals are simple, such as making an offering of lit candles, flowers, incense, food, or drink before an image of Buddha. In some traditions, such as in Tibetan Buddhism, the rituals are colorful and dramatic. During worship, Tibetan monks chant mantras, wear striking headdresses, blow horns, and use elaborate hand gestures. They often hold symbolic objects and bells.

At Tibetan festivals, there are often performances and dancing. Huge images on cloth may decorate temple walls, while intricate sand paintings called mandalas are created and destroyed. These dramatic rituals engage Buddhist followers emotionally and physically.

MANDALA SAND PAINTINGS

A mandala is a symbolic picture of the universe. It looks like a geometric pattern with various shapes, letters, and images. The mandala represents an imaginary palace, and each object stands for an aspect of wisdom or a reminder of a Buddhist principle. There are many different mandala designs, each focusing on a different lesson.

According to Buddhist teaching, mandalas bring about purification and healing to the people who view them. Often the mandala is created out of colored sand and displayed at festivals. After the festival, the mandala is destroyed, in keeping with the Buddhist idea that everything is temporary. By letting go of the image, followers accept detachment and move forward on their journey to enlightenment. You can see pictures of monks working on a mandala.

sand mandala creation

THE DALAI LAMA

The Dalai Lama is the spiritual leader of the Tibetan people, and Buddhists around the world follow his teachings. The word *dalai* translates from "ocean" in Mongolian and *lama* comes from "perfect teacher" in Tibetan Buddhism.

The first Dalai Lama was Gendun Drup (1391–1474). Buddhists believe that each Dalai Lama is a manifestation of Avalokiteshvara or Chenrezig, the Bodhisattva of Compassion and patron saint of Tibet. A bodhisattva is an enlightened being who has chosen to be reborn in order to help others reach enlightenment. According to Buddhist beliefs, each Dalai Lama is reincarnated from the previous one. When the Dalai Lama dies, a new one takes his place.

> When the 13th Dalai Lama died, religious leaders followed signs and visions and found a young child who lived near the Kumbum Monastery in Tibet.

This child, Lhamo Thondup (later called Tenzin Gyatso) born in 1935, became the 14th Dalai Lama. The Dalai Lama began his education as a Buddhist monk at age six. He studied intensely for many years and passed his final examination with honors. At age 23, the Dalai Lama was awarded the Geshe Lharampa degree, the equivalent of a doctorate of Buddhist philosophy.

The Chinese invaded Tibet in 1950, and the Dalai Lama fled to India in 1959, where he has lived ever since. He travels the world, sharing his beliefs in kindness and compassion. In 1989, the Dalai Lama received the Nobel Prize for Peace for his efforts to negotiate peace between Tibet and China.

Today, the vast majority of people practicing Buddhism live in the Asia-Pacific region, with 50 percent of them in China. For many of these followers, Buddhism is more than a religion. It can be thought of as a spiritual path that teaches its followers meditative practices that allow them to connect with their minds and free themselves from suffering.

BODH GAYA

Learn about Bodh Gaya, one of several sights in India associated with the birth of Buddhism.

🔍 Sacred Bodh Gaya

KEY QUESTIONS

- **What does Buddhism say about desire and craving? What does this mean for a society attracted to money and spending?**

- **How is the Buddhist idea of rebirth different than the Hindu idea of rebirth? How is meditation useful for followers of Buddhism? How is it useful for other people?**

COMPARE BUDDHISM AND HINDUISM IN A VENN DIAGRAM

The religions of Hinduism and Buddhism both originated in India. The founder of Buddhism came from a Hindu family. These religions have many similarities, yet are also very different.

In this activity, you will explore the similarities and differences of Hinduism and Buddhism and create a Venn diagram to visually display your findings. A Venn diagram uses overlapping circles to represent sets of information. The common elements of the two sets are placed in the overlapping section of the two circles.

- **Re-read the two chapters in this book on Hinduism and Buddhism.** What are some of the key elements, characteristics, and beliefs for each religion? Consider the following areas:

  1. Belief in God

  2. Worship practices

  3. Afterlife/ reincarnation

  4. Ritual practices

- **What did you find that is similar between the two religions?** What is different? Draw a Venn diagram to display your results. Place elements of each religion that you have learned in the appropriate circle and the common elements in the overlapping sections.

- **Share your diagram with your classmates.** How does your Venn diagram compare to your classmates' diagrams?

> To investigate more, add a third circle to your Venn diagram to represent your own religion. What areas are similar? What areas are different?

EXPLORE THE DALAI LAMA'S TEACHINGS

The Dalai Lama is a popular figure, even among people who don't practice Buddhism. He has written books and makes appearances all over the world. He even has his own website! You can find it here.

In this activity, you will explore some of the teachings of the Dalai Lama and see how they can be applied to modern life.

Explore the Dalai Lama's teachings on the Internet. You might find the following sites useful.

🔍 His Holiness, the 14th Dalai Lama of Tibet · The Dalai Lama's YouTube channel · The Private Dalai Lama

- **How can the teachings of the Dalai Lama be applied to your life?** Think about the following situations. How could the Dalai Lama's teachings be helpful in each scenario?

    1. You get a bad grade on a test.

    2. Several classmates are teasing another student because of his or her appearance.

    3. You attend a party where other teens are drinking and smoking.

    4. Your friend's father loses his job and the family is having financial trouble.

- **Present your answers to the class.** How do your answers compare to your classmates'? How were the answers similar? How were they different?

To investigate more, consider other ways the Dalai Lama's teachings could be applied to your life. Do you think his teachings are relevant in the modern world? Why or why not? Interview a member of the Buddhist faith to learn more about Buddhism and how its teachings apply to your life.

Ideas for Supplies ▼

- computer with Internet access
- mandala template
- chalk or pen and paper
- colored sand
- small funnel or drinking straw
- small paintbrush

CREATE A SAND MANDALA

Mandalas are beautiful, temporary representations of Buddhism. In this activity, you will design and create a sand mandala to experience this form of mindfulness and creativity.

- **Go online to find and print a template for a mandala design.** How can you modify the design?

- **Draw your mandala.** You can either draw it with chalk on the ground outside or with pen and paper.

- **Using the funnel or straw, draw lines of colored sand on the mandala and fill in the open spaces.** Be creative in your color choices and design ideas. Use the paintbrush to smooth the design and brush away extra pieces of sand.

- **Take your time to slowly and carefully complete your mandala.** Focus your mind on the process of creating, allowing your mind to clear itself of other distractions.

- **When you have completed the mandala, blow the sand away—make sure you do this outside!** According to Buddhist beliefs, the destruction of the mandala represents the impermanent nature of life.

> To investigate more, think about how it felt to destroy your artwork. Were you tempted to try to keep it? What does this teach you about desire and suffering?

DON'T SNEEZE!

Chapter 4
Christianity

What do followers of Christianity believe and what rituals do they follow?

With about 2.2 billion followers worldwide, Christianity is the world's largest religion. The word *Christianity* comes from *christos*, a Greek translation of the Hebrew word for "messiah" or "the anointed one." Christianity is based on the teachings of Jesus Christ, a Jewish preacher and healer who lived in the Middle East 2,000 years ago. A Jewish sect believed Jesus was the Messiah foretold in the Jewish Bible.

THE LIFE OF JESUS CHRIST

The history of Christianity begins with Jesus Christ. The birth, life, death, and resurrection of Jesus is recorded in four Gospels. These Gospels are included in the Christian Bible, the sacred text of this religion. According to the Gospels, Jesus of Nazareth was born in Bethlehem around 4 BCE during the reign of King Herod, who ruled Judea for the Roman Empire.

Christians believe Jesus Christ died to save people on Earth who believe in God, and they celebrate God through prayer and moral deeds.

In the Gospels, the angel Gabriel appeared to Mary and told her that she would conceive a child through the Holy Spirit, even though she was a virgin. On the night of Jesus's birth, a star appeared in the sky that led three wise men to a stable, where they believed they had found the "King of the Jews."

[
Shepherds in the fields witnessed an angel, who told them that a savior—the Messiah—had been born.
]

Little is known of Jesus's early life, but it is likely that he studied Jewish scriptures and religion as other Jewish children did. When he was about 30 years old, Jesus began his public ministry, teaching and spreading God's message. According to the Gospels, great crowds gathered to hear his stories and speeches. Jesus often spoke in parables, which are everyday stories that have a moral or spiritual message. Jesus used these parables to explain God and his kingdom.

SPLIT FROM JUDAISM

The belief that Jesus was the Messiah triggered the divide between Judaism and Christianity. Jesus's followers pointed to his resurrection as a sign that he was the true Messiah and could not be defeated by death. This belief contradicted Jewish laws. According to Jewish beliefs, humans cannot be divine and God cannot be human.

CRUCIFIXION

Several ancient societies, including ancient Rome, used crucifixion to put people to death. In a crucifixion, the condemned was tied or nailed to a large wooden cross. The victim was left to hang on the cross until he or she died. Public crucifixions sent a message warning people what could happen if they spoke out against society's rulers or did not obey its laws.

During the time that Jesus lived, Jerusalem was ruled by the Roman Empire. There were many tensions that existed between the Jews and Romans, both political and religious. Key Jewish religious texts promised that one day, God would send a king, the Messiah, to rule the world. The Jews believed that the Messiah would bring justice and peace to all, and he would free them from their Roman rulers to set up a kingdom where Jews would be their own rulers. The Jewish prophet Isaiah had claimed that when the Messiah came, his arrival would be marked by miracles of healing. The blind would see, the deaf would hear, and the crippled would walk.

When asked if he was the Messiah, Jesus insisted that he was an ordinary man, but stated that he spoke the word and will of God. Jesus's claim that he spoke with God's authority angered the Jewish authorities in Palestine. After he was betrayed by one of his disciples, the authorities arrested him. They accused him of blasphemy for claiming to be the son of God. They turned Jesus over to Roman authorities, who found him guilty of claiming to be the king of the Jews. This was a crime under Jewish law and treason under Roman law. The Romans convicted Jesus and sentenced him to death.

CRUCIFIXION AND RESURRECTION

After his conviction, Jesus was put to death by crucifixion. On a Friday, his body was placed in a tomb and an enormous stone was rolled in front of the tomb's entrance.

According to the Gospels, a group of women visited the tomb on the following Sunday and discovered that the stone had been moved and the tomb was empty. Two angels appeared to the women and told them that Jesus had risen from the dead. During the next 40 days, Jesus appeared to several of his disciples before rising to join God in heaven. The story of Jesus's death and resurrection is one of the foundations of the Christian religion.

> Christians believe that these events occurred to save those who believe in Jesus Christ and to show the promise of eternal life after death.

SPREAD OF CHRISTIANITY

After Jesus's death and resurrection, many of his disciples and followers believed he was the Messiah. While Jesus was alive on Earth, he had gathered 12 disciples to follow him and help him in his work. These men were known as the apostles. After Jesus's death, the apostles worked to spread the news of his resurrection, as well as his teachings about the love of God and love of one's neighbor.

At first, most people who believed that Jesus was the Messiah were Jews from Palestine. Within a few decades, however, the Christian message spread to non-Jews in surrounding areas. From these efforts, Christianity emerged.

SAINTS AND MARTYRS

In the Christian faith, men and women who die a martyr's death for their faith or live a life of extreme virtue are revered as saints. The word *saint* comes from the Latin word *sanctus*, which means "holy." Christians honor the memory of saints by making offerings, saying prayers, and petitioning the saints for special cures and miracles. They believe that the saints live in heaven with God and have special power to ask for God's help.

FACTS ON FAITH

The early persecution of Christians actually helped spread the word about Christianity by uniting Christians. Those put to death for their faith in Christianity were celebrated as martyrs.

Early Christians faced several obstacles. Because they refused to worship Greek and Roman gods or recognize the Roman emperor as a god, they were considered criminals and persecuted. Simply being a Christian was considered an act of treason. The Romans put many Christians to death for their beliefs, but still the religion grew in popularity. In 313 CE, the Roman emperor Constantine declared tolerance for all religions in the Roman Empire. By 392 CE, Christianity was declared to be the religion of the Roman Empire.

[Today, Christians live on every continent on Earth.]

THE HOLY TRINITY

Christianity is a monotheistic religion that believes in one God who is the eternal creator. Christians also believe that Jesus is the son of God, and that God became incarnate, or fully human, in Jesus. This idea, known as the Incarnation, is a central belief in Christianity.

The belief in Jesus as the son of God leads to the belief of the Holy Trinity. This is the idea that there is only one God, but that God exists in three distinct persons—the Father, the Son, and the Holy Spirit. God the Father sent Jesus to the world. Jesus, the son of God, came into the world to bring God's kingdom to Earth. The Holy Spirit aided Jesus on Earth and remains with Christians on Earth after Jesus returned to his Father. The Father, Son, and Holy Spirit are one, though each has a particular role.

According to the Gospel of John, Jesus told his followers that he would send the Holy Spirit to them after he had left them and returned to his Father in heaven. The Holy Spirit is said to transform the lives of Christian followers so that they can live the holy lives that God intends for them.

Christians believe that God sent Jesus to Earth in human form to bring God's kingdom from heaven to the earth.

JESUS'S TEACHINGS

In his teachings, Jesus frequently spoke about God's compassion and forgiveness. He emphasized mercy and kindness by saying, "Therefore all things whatsoever ye would that men should do to you, do ye even so to them . . . " (Matthew 7:12).

[Much of Jesus's teachings could be simply summarized as loving God and loving one's neighbor.]

Jesus also urged his followers to follow God's commandments. In the Old Testament, which comes from the Jewish Bible, the Ten Commandments received by Moses directly from God are a set of rules to guide moral behavior. The Ten Commandments refer to a person's relationship with God, parents, spouse, and community.

CHRISTIAN LOVE

Love is at the heart of many of Jesus's teachings. According to one story, when asked by a follower what the greatest commandment was, Jesus responded that his followers should love God with all their hearts. He said that the second greatest commandment was to love your neighbor as yourself.

The New Testament not only includes the four Gospels but also a book called the Acts of the Apostles, which tells the story of how Christianity spread from a small group of Jesus's disciples to many people around the world.

According to the Gospel of Matthew, Jesus also shared a series of blessings for right behavior, called the Beatitudes, during his Sermon on the Mount. The Beatitudes state qualities that Christians should try to show in order to live a blessed life and gain eternal life with God in heaven. These qualities include humility, simplicity, righteousness, purity of heart, mercy, peace-making, and a readiness to endure persecution for being a Christian. The Sermon on the Mount also introduced one of Christianity's key prayers, the Lord's Prayer, sometimes called the Our Father.

CHRISTIANITY'S GOAL: SALVATION

By acknowledging Jesus as the son of God and following his teachings, Christians hope to achieve their spiritual goal of salvation, a state of redemption and reconciliation with God. The path to salvation differs by denomination. Protestants believe that salvation is achieved solely through faith and the acceptance of Jesus Christ. Roman Catholics and Eastern Orthodox Christians believe that salvation also depends on faith in the church's mysteries and on the fulfillment of sacraments, or religious ceremonies.

Although the path to salvation may differ, Christians believe that humans have immortal souls and that there is an eternal life after death. After the physical body dies, the human soul lives on forever. This belief varies slightly among the many Christian denominations, but the majority believe that after death, followers of Christ go to heaven to live in the presence of God and others who died before. The Christian view of heaven is a place free of sin, suffering, and pain.

Many Christians also believe in hell, a place of punishment that is the opposite of heaven because people are deprived of God there. The souls of those who do not achieve salvation are damned to spend eternity in hell. In the New Testament, the Bible describes hell as a place with fire. Some Christians interpret this description literally and believe that people in hell feel as though they are burning. Others believe the fire is symbolic of severe, painful punishment.

THE BIBLE

The Bible is the sacred text of Christianity and contains stories, songs, poetry, letters, and historical accounts. Christians believe that the Bible was inspired by God. The Christian Bible differs from the Jewish Bible by having two sections—the Old Testament and the New Testament.

The Old Testament is the original Jewish Bible, although the books of the sacred scripture of Judaism are ordered in a slightly different way. The Old Testament was written during many years and contains stories about the relationship between God and his chosen people, offers examples of how people are meant to live, and includes sayings and stories of the prophets as well as writings such as psalms and proverbs.

The New Testament was written by Christians in the first century CE. It has 27 books that can be divided into two main sections. The four Gospels, written by Matthew, Mark, Luke, and John, tell the story of Jesus. While the four Gospels agree on many details, there are some differences in how the writers chronicle Jesus's life. The Letters, or Epistles, in the New Testament are written by Christian leaders to give guidance to early Christian followers.

The Bible has been translated into more than 2,000 languages.

ORIGINAL SIN

All Christians believe that the failure of Adam and Eve to obey God in the Garden of Eden introduced sin into the world. This idea developed into the concept of original sin, in which every human being is born with a piece of Adam's sin.

Some Christians also recognize the Seven Deadly Sins as the source of all other sin. These sins are pride, greed, lust, anger, gluttony, envy, and sloth.

There are more than 400 Christian denominations.

PILGRIMAGES

Every year, thousands of Christians travel to places associated with the life of Christ, such as Bethlehem, Jerusalem, and Galilee. Other popular pilgrimage sites for Catholics are places where visitations of the Virgin Mary have occurred, such as Fatima in Portugal and Lourdes in France. You can explore the following websites to learn more about the history of Fatima and Lourdes and the visions of Mary that have appeared at each site, see pictures of the shrines, and watch live video footage from the sites.

Virgin Mary Fatima pilgrimage Lourdes vision

Church leaders used the Epistles as a way to communicate with early Christians. They offer advice to people about how to express their commitment to Jesus and belief in Christianity.

The Bible has been interpreted in different ways by the many Christian denominations. Fundamentalist Christians believe that every word of the Bible is inspired by God and should be followed literally. For example, many fundamentalist women wear only skirts, because the Bible says in Deuteronomy 22:5, "The woman shall not wear that which pertaineth unto a man, neither shall a man put on a woman's garment: for all that do so are abomination unto the LORD thy God." Other Christians view the Bible less as a literal text and more as an allegory, which can be interpreted to reveal hidden meanings.

CHRISTIAN DENOMINATIONS

Through the years, hundreds of Christian denominations or groups have emerged. While there is much similarity among the many Christian branches, there are also differences in beliefs, worship practices, and holidays. The three largest branches are Roman Catholic, Eastern Orthodox, and Protestant.

The largest branch of Christianity is Roman Catholicism. The pope, also known as the Bishop of Rome, is the leader of the Catholic Church. Catholics consider St. Peter, one of Jesus's 12 apostles, to be the first pope. Roman Catholic worship is elaborate, with special ceremonies or rites called sacraments. Saints are an important part of Roman Catholic worship. Catholic churches are led by ordained priests, who are unmarried.

While similar to Roman Catholicism in many ways, Eastern Orthodoxy does not follow the pope. Instead, it is led by bishops and councils.

In addition, Eastern Orthodox priests can marry before they are ordained as priests. Orthodox worship focuses on sacraments and the use of sacred images called icons.

In the sixteenth century, a group of Christian leaders protested against many parts of the Roman Catholic Church, including the authority of the pope. Protestantism developed from this division and became an extremely diverse branch of Christianity, with a number of denominations, worship styles, types of governance, types of ministers, and beliefs. Protestant denominations include Congregational, Methodist, Baptist, Presbyterian, Lutheran, Mormon, and many, many more. Most Protestant churches are led by ministers, who in many denominations can be married. In some Protestant churches, women can be ordained as ministers.

PRAYER AND WORSHIP

While Christians can worship and pray alone, much of Christian worship takes place in a church, which is considered an essential element to the faith. Christian worship grew out of Jewish traditions and is modeled after early gatherings at synagogues. While the Jewish Sabbath is on Saturday, Christians celebrate Sunday as the holy day of rest and worship. Sunday is the day of the week that Jesus is said to have risen from the dead.

Christians are expected to attend church services weekly. These services, called a Mass by some denominations, involve hymns, a sermon, readings from scriptures, recitation of prayers, and other holy ceremonies or sacraments. Church services vary by church and denomination. Some are elaborate events, with choirs and musicians. Others use simpler hymns and rely on the congregation to sing.

Christians have numerous rituals to honor God and the life of Jesus. Rituals include readings from the Bible, prayers, vigils, fasts, and pilgrimages.

FACTS ON FAITH

At the Last Supper, Jesus ate bread and drank wine and told his disciples to eat the bread and drink the wine in memory of him.

In some Christian denominations, the weekly service includes a sacrament called the Eucharist. The Eucharist is a re-enactment of the Last Supper, the final meal that Jesus shared with his disciples before his arrest and crucifixion. At a Mass, the priest recites specific prayers and readings. Followers celebrate the Eucharist by taking a sip of consecrated wine and consuming a piece of bread called Holy Communion.

While many Christian denominations celebrate the Eucharist, they have different interpretations about its meaning. For Roman Catholics, the bread and wine used during Mass are transformed into the actual body and blood of Christ. They believe that although the bread and wine remain physically the same, their substance becomes Jesus. Roman Catholics believe that receiving the Eucharist is the most important act of worship and it should be received at least weekly, during Mass. Other Christian denominations participate in the Eucharist as a symbolic memory of an event in the life of Jesus.

Many Christians also participate in baptism, an initiation ritual in which a person is accepted into the church. Some denominations baptize infants, while others baptize adults. In a baptism, a person has water poured over their head or is totally immersed in water, which symbolizes their sins being washed away.

In Roman Catholic and Eastern Orthodox churches, there are five additional sacraments. These include confirmation, which seals one with the gift of the Holy Spirit; penance, where a person atones for their sins; marriage; holy orders; and anointing of the sick. Catholics and Orthodox Christians believe that these sacraments are signs of grace given by Jesus.

CHURCHES

Many Christians do much of their worshiping in churches. The design of churches has changed through the years, but a few elements have remained constant. Have you ever been inside a church? What is it about the architecture that makes it feel different from other buildings?

During the Middle Ages, many Christian churches were built in the form of a cross. Two side areas, called transepts, intersect and lead off the church's main long body, which is called the nave. Solid stone, vaulted ceilings, soaring spires, and light made the church a place of reverence and awe, and reminded worshipers of their relationship with God and the promise of salvation.

The date of Easter Sunday is determined each year by the Sunday after the first full moon that falls either on or after March 21.

In 1054, differences in beliefs between the Eastern (Greek) and Western (Roman) branches of Christianity led to the Great Schism. A key factor in the division was the role of the pope. In the Western churches, followers revered the pope as the church's supreme spiritual leader. The Eastern churches, however, refused to accept the pope and insisted that spiritual authority should remain with all the church's bishops. The Great Schism led to the separate development of the Orthodox Church and the Roman Catholic Church.

FACTS ON FAITH

Purple is a symbolic color used in some churches throughout Lent. Purple is associated with mourning and represents the pain and suffering of Jesus's crucifixion. Purple is also the color associated with royalty.

With a focus on light and uplifting space, the design of many medieval churches is based on symbolism and geometric harmony. The entrance is often placed in the west, representing the setting sun, darkness, and death. The altar is located at the church's eastern end, in the direction of the rising sun, light, and resurrection.

Most churches have an altar, chancel, nave, pulpit, and pews. Many churches also have stained glass, which fills the church's interior with colored light. The shape and proportion of these windows can have meaning. For example, groups of three represent the Trinity and groups of four represents the Gospels and their authors. Christian churches typically include many sacred images, including sculptures, paintings, mosaics, frescoes, carved altar pieces, and stained glass. These pieces often represent the sacred people and stories of Christianity.

HOLIDAYS

Christians celebrate several holy days and holidays throughout the year. Two of the more important holidays are Christmas and Easter.

Celebrated every year on December 25 (or January 7 for Orthodox Christians), Christmas commemorates the birth of Jesus, known as the Nativity. The New Testament describes Jesus's birth as taking place in a manger in the city of Bethlehem. Christians prepare to celebrate Christmas during a four-week period called Advent. Churches decorate with Advent wreaths, which contain four candles, and each Sunday during Advent, one of the candles is lit. On Christmas Day, Christians celebrate by going to church, exchanging gifts, and preparing special meals for family and friends.

The most important Christian holiday is Easter Sunday, which commemorates the resurrection of Jesus Christ. The date of Easter changes each year, but always occurs in the spring. For 40 days before Easter, many Christians reflect, pray, and prepare during a period called Lent. While Easter is a celebration of Jesus's resurrection, Lent serves as a reminder of the events leading up to Jesus's death on the cross. Christians who observe Lent use it as a time for prayer and penance. It is common for Christians to give up a favorite food or bad habit for the duration of Lent in recognition of Jesus's sacrifices.

The week preceding Easter Sunday is known as Holy Week. It features special services and rituals on Palm Sunday to recall Jesus's entry into Jerusalem, on Holy Thursday to mark the Last Supper, and on Good Friday to remember Jesus's crucifixion and death. Holy Week ends with Easter Sunday.

Although his life was short, Jesus Christ's message of hope, compassion, and eternal life resonated with people around the world. It spread quickly from person to person, and nation to nation. Its reach extended far and wide across the entire world. Today, about 2.2 billion people, or one in every three people, call themselves Christian.

KEY QUESTIONS

- **The idea of eternal life is a central belief of Christianity. Why do you think this idea is attractive to people?**

- **Why did some Jewish people believe that Jesus Christ was the Messiah? Why did others not agree?**

- **What is the Trinity, according to Christian belief? How is this idea monotheistic?**

FACTS ON FAITH

Ash Wednesday marks the beginning of Lent for Western Christian churches. Some Christian churches hold special services where each person is marked with ashes on the forehead as symbols of repentance.

FACTS ON FAITH

State funerals for three U.S. Presidents have been held at the National Cathedral: Dwight Eisenhower (1969), Ronald Reagan (2004), and Gerald Ford (2007).

ARCHITECTURE AND THE NATIONAL CATHEDRAL IN WASHINGTON, DC

In 1907, builders laid the first foundation stone for the National Cathedral in Washington, DC. Although the Bethlehem Chapel at the cathedral opened for services in 1912, the cathedral remained under construction for 83 years. It was finally completed in 1990. A cathedral of the Episcopal Church, the National Cathedral is the sixth-largest cathedral in the world and the second-largest in the United States. The design of the National Cathedral reflects many elements of Christianity. In this activity, you will explore the National Cathedral and investigate how its design reflects the Christian faith.

- **Explore the National Cathedral on the Internet.** You can start with the cathedral's website.

National Cathedral Washington and history

- **Identify elements of the cathedral's design that have meaning in Christianity.** Consider the following questions.

  - What is the shape of the cathedral? What do the soaring arches represent?

  - How do the cathedral's decorative art and sculptures represent Christian beliefs?

- **Make a presentation on what you have learned for your classmates, family, and friends.**

To investigate more, imagine that you are going to design a Christian church. What elements would you include in your design? Why?

INTERPRET A PARABLE

Jesus used many parables in his teachings. A parable is a simple story that explains God's kingdom and includes a moral lesson. One of his most famous parables told the story of the Good Samaritan. In this activity, you will read the parable of the Good Samaritan and investigate its meaning for Christians.

- **Find and read the Parable of the Good Samaritan in the Bible (Luke 10:25–37).** If you do not have access to a Bible, you can find this parable online.

🔍 parable Good Samaritan

- **What lessons does this parable illustrate?** How did Jesus use this story to show his followers how he wanted them to act? What details from the story support your answer?

- **Think about how this parable applies to modern life.** What situations can you think of that present a similar situation? Do parables from the Bible have meaning in today's world?

> To investigate more, write your own short parable. Have a friend or classmate read it and discuss their interpretation of it. What meaning did they find in your parable? How did it compare to the meaning you intended for the parable?

VOCAB LAB 📖

Write down what you think each word means: **resurrection**, **ministry**, **miracles**, **blasphemy**, **crucifixion**, **martyr**, **apostles**, **persecution**, **allegory**, and **baptism**.

Compare your definitions with those of your friends or classmates. Did you all come up with the same meanings? Turn to the text and glossary if you need help.

THANKS FOR BEING A GOOD SAMARITAN!

COMPARE CREATION STORIES

Every religion has its own story to explain the origins of the world and mankind. In this activity, you will investigate and compare creation stories from Christianity, Hinduism, and Buddhism.

🔍 Genesis creation story Bible · Hindu creation story · Buddhist creation story

- **Find and read the Christian and Jewish creation story in the first two chapters of Genesis in the Bible.** If you do not have access to a Bible, you can find this text above.

- **Now, watch a video of a Hindu creation story from the first chapter of this book.**

- **Watch a video of a Buddhist creation story.**

- **Compare the different creation stories.** How are they similar? How are they different? How does each incorporate elements of their respective faiths? Why do you think creation stories have similarities?

> To investigate more, read a creation story from another faith. How does it compare to the creation stories you have already studied?

Chapter 5
Islam

What do the followers
of Islam believe
and how do they
practice their faith?

Followers of Islam, who are called Muslims, believe that there is one true God, Allah. Muslims live according to His laws.

Followers of Islam believe that theirs is an ancient faith that has always existed as God's chosen religion. Islam traces its roots back to several prophets who are also recognized by other religions. Abraham, who is considered by Jews to be the father of Judaism, is believed to be one in a long line of prophets sent by God to reveal the true faith of Islam. Other prophets include Moses and David from Judaism and Christianity and Jesus from Christianity. The last prophet, the prophet Muhammad, established the Islamic religion.

Like Judaism and Christianity, Islam is a monotheistic religion. Followers believe there is only one God. Some Muslims call him Allah. Islam, which means "submission to the will of God" in Arabic, teaches that in order to achieve true peace, followers must submit to God and live according to His laws. The word *Muslim* means "one who submits to the will of God."

There are more than 1.6 billion Muslims, approximately 23 percent of the world's population, worldwide. The majority of Muslims—62 percent—live in the Asia-Pacific region. Many Muslims also live in the Middle East and North Africa (20 percent) and sub-Saharan Africa (16 percent). The remaining Muslims are scattered in Europe, North America, Latin America, and the Caribbean.

> Muslims believe that Islam is not a new religion because it has always been the only acceptable religion in the eyes of God.

All of God's prophets, including Abraham, Noah, Moses, Jesus, and Muhammad, carried the same message: Nothing should be worshiped except Allah, and all human beings should submit to His will.

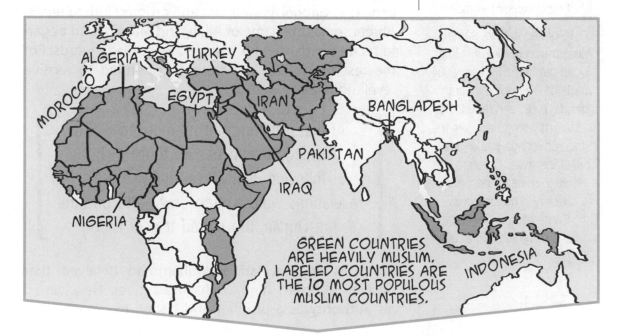

ALGERIA TURKEY
MOROCCO EGYPT IRAN BANGLADESH
PAKISTAN
IRAQ
NIGERIA
GREEN COUNTRIES ARE HEAVILY MUSLIM. LABELED COUNTRIES ARE THE 10 MOST POPULOUS MUSLIM COUNTRIES.
INDONESIA

The prophet Muhammad is not considered the founder of Islam. Instead, he is the final prophet. When Muhammad received God's final and complete revelation of faith, God fulfilled the covenant that He had made centuries earlier with Abraham.

THE PROPHET MUHAMMAD

The Islamic tradition can be traced to the town of Mecca, which is in today's Saudi Arabia, in the seventh century CE. Born about 570 CE and orphaned at an early age, Muhammad lived in Mecca with his uncle's family. According to Islamic history, around 582 CE, a Christian hermit named Bahira noticed Muhammad and determined that he carried the sign of prophecy.

As an adult, Muhammad was surrounded by claims about God from the Jews, Christians, and polytheists. In 610, he climbed Mount Hira near Mecca to meditate and search for the truth about God. One night, as Muhammad meditated in a cave, the angel Jibreel, also known as Gabriel, visited him and ordered him to recite. Jibreel spoke the name of Allah, and Muhammad began to recite words that he believed were God's words. For the rest of his life, Muhammad continued to receive revelations from God.

> At first, Muhammad memorized God's revelations and passed them to his followers orally. Eventually, these revelations were written down and became the Qur'an, the sacred text of Islam.

After his first revelation, Muhammad believed that God had chosen him as His messenger. He claimed his authority as a prophet and began to preach what

HIJAB

In Islam, hijab is the custom of dressing and behaving modestly for both men and women. In some places, Muslim women are required to observe hijab in front of any man they could possibly marry. This does not include a woman's father, brothers, grandfathers, uncles, or young children. Hijab does not need to be worn in front of other Muslim women.

To observe hijab, some Muslim women dress in long, loose garments that cover all parts of the body except the hands, face, and feet. Other Muslim women also wear face coverings that expose only their eyes. Others cover only their head, hair, and chest with headscarves. Some Muslim women don't observe hijab at all.

God had revealed to him. He taught that there was no God but Allah, and therefore people should live in complete submission to the will of Allah. Many people in the town of Mecca believed Muhammad's message, but they were persecuted for their beliefs.

In 622, Muhammad and his followers left Mecca and settled in the nearby northern town of Medina. Today, this journey is known as the Hijrah, or migration. In Medina, Muhammad established the first Islamic city-state. He became Medina's spiritual, political, and military leader.

Muhammad continued to preach God's message and his followers grew in number. Ten years after leaving Mecca, Muhammad returned and conquered the city. He established the beginnings of an Islamic empire that would unite the separate tribes of Arabia. Muhammad died that same year, in 632.

NO GOD BUT ALLAH

The foundation of Islam is the monotheistic belief in one Almighty God, the same God of Abraham, Moses, and Jesus. Islam teaches that God is loving, compassionate, merciful, and concerned with the daily lives of humans.

Although Muslims worship the same God as Jews and Christians, their concept of God is slightly different. The Islamic God is based entirely on Divine Revelations from God to the prophets.

In addition, in Islam there is no ambiguity about God's divinity. Simply stated, God is God and man is man. Muslims believe that God is the only creator of the world, and He and His creation never mix. According to this belief, Islam rejects the Christian belief in the Trinity.

FACTS ON FAITH

The Qur'an is the book of sacred writings accepted by Muslims as revelations made to Muhammad by Allah through the angel Jibreel. The Sunna is the body of Islamic custom and practice based on Muhammad's words and deeds.

SHARI'A

After Muhammad's death, the Muslim community established a government and set of laws based on the Qur'an and the Sunna. This law, known as the Shari'a, applies to all individual and community activities. Shari'a law provides the rules for living a righteous life. The guardian of the Shari'a laws was the caliph, the religious and political leader of the Muslim community.

THE SPREAD OF ISLAM

After Muhammad's death in the year 632, Islam quickly spread through trade routes, migrating people, and conquest. Muhammad's successor was his close companion and father-in-law, Abu Bakr. Known as the first caliph, or successor, Abu Bakr consolidated Arabia into a single united country under Muslim control.

Subsequent caliphs spread Islam throughout the Middle East and into parts of Egypt, Anatolia, and Armenia. Within a century of Mohammad's death, the Islamic Empire reached across northern African and into parts of Asia.

Today, Islam has become one of the world's largest religions, practiced by nearly one-fourth of the world's people. About 50 countries have a majority of people who are Muslim, including Saudi Arabia, Afghanistan, Pakistan, and Iran.

THE HADITH

The Hadith, or Sunna, is an Islamic text that records Muhammad's words, called hadith, and his actions, called sunna. This text is accepted as a commentary on what the Qur'an means and how it should be applied. The Hadith guides Muslims on how to live their daily lives.

> Many other countries, particularly in the Middle East, have designated Islam as the official state religion.

SACRED TEXT: THE QUR'AN

God's revelations to Muhammad were written down in the Qur'an, the sacred text of Islam. Muslims believe the Qur'an is the sacred word of God, and that it confirms God's message previously printed in other sacred texts, such as the Jewish Torah and the Christian Bible's New Testament. The verses of the Qur'an, called the ayat, reveal what God commands.

The standard version of the Qur'an was written down shortly after Muhammad's death. The Qur'an contains 114 chapters, each written in Arabic. They are arranged by length, with the longer chapters at the beginning and the shorter chapters at the end. The chapters cover a wide range of topics, providing guidance on worship, politics, marriage, family life, care for the poor, hygiene, community, and economics. Many chapters are named for the story, theme, or truth that they reveal.

Muslims who are able to memorize the entire Qur'an earn great prestige and blessings. A Muslim who is able to accomplish this memorization is called a hafiz, or guardian of the Qur'an. Why do you think Muslims value memorization of a sacred text? Does a poem or song change its meaning for you when you memorize it?

Muslims treat the Qur'an with great respect, as they believe it is the direct word of God. They follow several guidelines when handling it. The Qur'an should never be left on the floor or in any unclean place.

FACTS ON FAITH

Portions of the Qur'an were written on animal bone, leather, stones, palm leaves, and parchment.

THE QUR'AN

The Qur'an has been translated into more than 40 languages. You can read an English translation of the Qur'an at this website.

🔍 Qur'an English translation

FACTS ON FAITH

In order to avoid idolatry, Islam tradition forbids illustrations within the Qur'an. Patterns are permitted, and beautiful calligraphy is often used to write out the Qur'an's text with colored inks and gold leaf.

PILGRIMAGE TO MECCA

About 2 million people might make the pilgrimage to Mecca, Muhammad's birthplace, in any year. It's a trip that holds great meaning for Muslims. You can watch a video about this pilgrimage. Is there any place in your life that might hold similar meaning for you?

🔍 Mecca Muslim pilgrimage

In addition, Muslim tradition says that Muslims should ritually clean themselves before handling the Qur'an. They also should be extremely careful when carrying the holy book and follow specific disposal guidelines for old, worn-out copies of the holy book. What does this level of care tell you about how Muslims feel about the Qur'an?

FIVE PILLARS OF ISLAM

According to Islamic tradition, the prophet Muhammad summarized Islam in five principles. These principles are known as the Five Pillars of Islam.

Today, all branches of Islam accept these five principles as the core of the Islamic faith. Muslims believe that they must live by these Five Pillars in order to live a good Islamic life.

- **Shahada** – saying that there is only one God and Muhammad is his messenger
- **Salat** – performing ritual prayers
- **Zakat** – giving to charity
- **Sawm** – fasting during the month of Ramadan
- **Hajj** – making a pilgrimage to Mecca

The first pillar, shahada, requires Muslims to acknowledge that there is one true God and that Muhammad is his messenger. At birth, the shahada is whispered in a baby's ear. It is also whispered in a Muslim's ear at death.

[The shahada is spoken by Muslims as testimony several times throughout the day.]

The second pillar is salat, or prayer. Muslims are summoned to prayer five times every day—at dawn, noon, mid-afternoon, dusk, and evening. Often, Muslims gather at a mosque for prayer, but prayers can be performed alone or in groups in other locations. All Muslims are called to prayer and even children as young as seven are encouraged to pray.

The third pillar is zakat, or charity. Muslims are called to care for their communities, not only through acts of charity, but also by paying an alms tax. Adult Muslims are encouraged to offer a percentage of their assets for this tax, typically 2.5 percent.

> Giving alms demonstrates the Muslim belief that everything they have comes from God and that they should give to those who have received less.

The fourth pillar, sawm, calls for Muslims to fast during Ramadan. This is a month-long spiritual celebration that commemorates the time that Muhammad received his first revelation from the angel Jibreel.

The fifth pillar is hajj, which calls on Muslims to make a pilgrimage to the holy city of Mecca. Every adult Muslim who is physically and financially able should travel to Mecca at least once in his or her lifetime.

Hajj takes place after the month of Ramadan. Muslims gather together in Mecca during the hajj, perform acts of worship, and praise Allah together. This pilgrimage intends to promote the bonds of Islam by showing that every Muslim is equal in Allah's eyes.

FACTS ON FAITH

The call to prayer is made from the top of the mosque by a person known as a muezzin.

Mosques are built with a minaret rising above the structure. The minaret tower is where the call to prayer was traditionally made from.

Once in Mecca, pilgrims visit the Kaaba, a cube-shaped structure at the center of Mecca's Grand Mosque. According to Islamic tradition, the Kaaba was built by Abraham and his son, Ismail (Ishmael), to serve as the house of God. Before arriving at the Kaaba, Muslims purify themselves and dress in simple clothing.

PRAYER AND WORSHIP

Prayer is an important part of Islamic worship. Salat, the second pillar of Islam, requires Muslims to pray five times a day. The ritual of daily prayer has been practiced for more than 1,400 years and is repeated by millions of people around the world.

Islamic prayer unites mind, soul, and body, so Muslims perform a series of movements with the words of each prayer. To pray, Muslims stand facing the direction of Mecca and recite the prayers. In Muslim countries, such as Pakistan, Turkey, and Afghanistan, mosques issue a public call to prayer, called the adhan, through loudspeakers.

Many Muslims worship in a mosque, the center of Islamic worship. While Muslims can pray individually, they are encouraged to pray with others in a mosque. A specially decorated niche within a mosque, called a mihrab, marks the direction of Mecca.

> In addition to being a prayer space, mosques are used for meetings, teachings, and study.

Muslims who pray outside a mosque generally use a special prayer mat, so that their prayers are always performed in a clean place. Everyone is welcome to pray at the mosque.

Traditionally, men and women pray separately and in some mosques, there is a special area designated for women.

Before prayer, Muslims perform a ritual washing called wudhu. Muslims believe that they should be clean and dressed in good clothes before presenting themselves before Allah. Wudhu involves washing parts of the body such as the hands, mouth, nose, face, arms, hair, and feet in a specific order and number of times. Most mosques have washing facilities for Muslims to use before praying.

RAMADAN

The month of Ramadan, celebrated during the ninth month of the Islamic calendar, is a special time of prayer and fasting. Muslims believe that this month has been blessed by Allah, and therefore good actions and prayer during Ramadan bring greater reward.

Many Muslims try to give up bad habits during Ramadan, resolve to pray more, and recite the Qur'an. Many mosques recite parts of the Qur'an each night.

THE AFTERLIFE

Muslims believe in an afterlife. They believe that after death, the soul is examined by two of God's angels. Then, on the final Day of Judgment, God judges all humans and holds them accountable for how they have used the gift of life. True believers who have followed his word will be brought into paradise, while those who have not obeyed God's word will be cast into hell.

During Ramadan, Muslims refrain from food, drink, and sexual intimacy during the daylight hours. Instead, they use the daytime to purify themselves and reflect upon their spiritual condition. Each morning before dawn, families gather to eat small meals. After dark, they have larger meals that often include dates, which Muhammad is said to have eaten to break his fast.

During Ramadan, many Muslims also go to the mosque for special evening prayers. They recite a special prayer said only during Ramadan.

Ramadan marks the month in which the Qur'an was first revealed to the prophet Muhammad. It is also believed to be the time when the gates of heaven are opened and the gates of hell are closed.

HOLY DAYS

Ramadan ends with a special feast called Eid al-Fitr, which ends the month of fasting. According to Islamic tradition, the prophet Muhammad celebrated the first Eid in 624 CE with friends and family to mark the end of fasting and to thank Allah for the help and strength he provided during Ramadan. This is the same reason Muslims celebrate Eid al-Fitr today!

To celebrate, families visit each other, share special meals, and exchange gifts and sweets. The celebrations can run for several days.

Another Islamic holy day, called Eid al-Adha, or the festival of sacrifice, remembers the prophet Abraham's, or Ibrahim's, willingness to obey God and sacrifice his own son. This demonstrated Ibrahim's complete submission to God's will. In the Islamic version of the story, Ibrahim's son even grants his father permission to perform the sacrifice.

[The celebrations remind Muslims of their own submission to Allah.]

During the holiday, Muslims sacrifice domestic animals, typically sheep, to symbolize Ibrahim's sacrifice. The meat is given to family, friends, and the poor in one-third shares. Muslims also celebrate the festival with prayers and presents.

JIHAD

In the Islamic faith, the concept of jihad, according to the Qur'an, has many meanings. In general, jihad is the idea of working toward a perfect moral order in society and in individual life. It calls every Muslim to struggle against anything that might corrupt God's word. This struggle can refer to internal efforts to be a good Muslim or working to inform others about the Islamic faith.

While jihad allows the use of force to protect the faith against others if no peaceful means are successful, it has strict rules. Innocents such as women, children, and the sick should never be harmed, and any peaceful solutions should be accepted. In recent years, some extremist groups have used the word jihad to justify violence. Many Islamic scholars say that this is a misuse of jihad, because violence goes against the teachings of Islam.

ISLAMIC LEADERS

In Islam, there are no clergy members. All followers are on equal footing as human beings with no religious middlemen standing between the individual and God. An imam acts as the leader of a Muslim community and leads the Friday prayer.

Today, the majority of the world's Muslims are Sunni Muslims.

DIVISIONS OF ISLAM

When Muhammad died in 632 CE, he had no sons. The Muslim community was divided over who should succeed Muhammad as their leader. The majority of Muslims thought that the most qualified man should become the next leader, or caliph.

They chose Abu Bakr, a companion of the prophet, because he had been closely guided by Muhammad. The majority of Muslims supported the idea of electing the best leader, which was in line with the teachings of Muhammad. Supporters of Bakr became known as the Sunni Muslims.

A small group of Muslims disagreed with the election of Bakr as the new leader. This group, who became Shi'a Muslims, believed that a close relative of Muhammad's should be caliph. They believed that Muhammad himself had appointed his son-in-law and cousin, Ali, to lead the Muslim community.

One of the main differences between the Sunni and Shi'a Muslims is the Shi'a belief in a line of leaders known as imams. Shi'a Muslims believe that the imams were descendants of Muhammad through Ali and are the only legitimate authority on Earth. This line of imams ended in the ninth century.

[Today, the division between the Sunni and Shi'a Muslims continues.]

Islam is the fastest-growing religion and might someday be the largest. The more people can learn about the history and culture of different religions, the better they'll be able to understand and accept all members of the human population, despite their differences.

KEY QUESTIONS

- In what ways is Islam connected to Judaism and Christianity? In what ways is it different?

- What does it mean that Muslims believe that Islam is not a new religion?

- Why are there no illustrations in the Qur'an or depictions of God in Islamic art? How does this relate to the Islamic concept of God?

INTERVIEW A MUSLIM IMAM, A JEWISH RABBI, AND A CHRISTIAN PRIEST OR MINISTER

One of the best ways to understand and compare different religions or faiths is to talk directly with people who are members of those faiths. In this activity, you will discuss the Islamic, Jewish, and Christian faiths directly with people who practice them.

- **Identify people who practice Islam, Judaism, and Christianity whom you can interview.** Schedule times to meet or talk over the phone with each.

- **Before the interview, spend some time thinking about questions that you have about each religion.** What would you like to learn more about? What interests you about the religion?

- **Conduct the interviews at the scheduled times.** During the interviews, do some of the person's answers spark new questions?

- **After the interviews, think about the following questions.**

  1. What have you learned about the three religions that you did not know previously?

  2. What was the most surprising thing you learned about each religion?

  3. How do Islam, Judaism, and Christianity compare with each other? How do they compare with your religion if it's different? If you do not practice a religion, think about how it compares with aspects of your life. What similarities are there? What differences exist?

> To investigate more, compare these interviews with the interviews you conducted with people of the Hindu and Buddhist faiths. What similarities did you find among the religions? What differences?

To investigate more, imagine that you are going to design a Muslim mosque. What elements would you include in your design? Why?

ARCHITECTURE AND MOSQUES

For Muslims, the mosque is a gathering place for prayer. The Arabic name for mosque is masjid, which means "place of prostration." All Muslim men are required to gather at the mosque for the Friday noon prayer. The prophet Muhammad lived in the first mosque, which had a large courtyard that was surrounded by long rooms. Columns lined the rooms. This style of mosque was called a hypostyle mosque, which means "many columns."

In this activity, you will explore the elements of the architecture of a mosque and their meanings in the Islamic faith.

* **Do some research on the different types of mosques and the meanings of common elements.** You can find information at the following websites.

🔍 mosque architecture • Blue Mosque design

* **Investigate the Blue Mosque, a famous mosque in Turkey.**

* **Identify elements of the Blue Mosque's design that have meaning in Islam.** To get you starting thinking about this, consider these questions.

  1. What is the purpose or significance of the minaret?

  2. What type of decoration is found in a mosque? Why?

* **Present what you have learned to your classmates, family, and friends.**

UNDERSTANDING SACRED TEXTS: THE QUR'AN AND THE CHRISTIAN BIBLE

The Qur'an is the sacred text of Islam. Muslims believe that God revealed his messages directly to the prophet Muhammad and they were later recorded by his followers in the Qur'an. Muhammad is believed to be the last in a series of prophets who received God's message.

Jesus Christ, whom Christians believe to be the Messiah and son of God, is considered a prophet in the Islamic faith. In this activity, you will analyze a section of the Qur'an that talks about the baby Jesus and his mother, Mary (Maryam in Islam).

- **Read Surah 19:16–34 in the Qur'an.** You can find a translation of this text online.

Qur'an Surah 19:16–34 • Bible Luke 1:26–37 • Bible Luke 2:1–35

- **After reading this text, compare it to a similar story in the Christian Bible in the New Testament in Luke 1:26–37 and Luke 2:1–35.** You can find these sections above.

- **What similarities do the two stories share?** What differences are there? How does each support the beliefs of its faith? How do the stories reflect the values of the followers of each religion?

To investigate more, select another section of the Qur'an to read. What message does it have for followers of Islam? How is this message similar to those contained in sacred texts from other religions? How is it different?

COMPARING ABRAHAM IN THREE SACRED TEXTS

Judaism, Christianity, and Islam are called the Abrahamic faiths. Each considers Abraham to be an important figure in the development of the faith. In the sacred text of each religion, there are stories of Abraham and his relationship with God. In this activity, you will compare how each religion's sacred text presents the story of Abraham and Isaac.

• **Read the story of Abraham and Isaac in each sacred text.** If you do not have copies of the Qur'an, Christian Bible, and Jewish Torah, you can find these stories online.

Qur'an 37:100–109 · Torah Genesis 22:1–18 · Bible Genesis 22:1–18

• **What similarities do the three accounts share?** What differences are there? How does each support the beliefs of its faith? Why is Abraham an important figure in each faith?

> To investigate more, think about how Judaism, Christianity, and Islam trace the origins of their religions to Abraham but diverge after Abraham. What caused each to take a different path? How did this result in different beliefs? You can draw a Venn diagram to illustrate the similarities and differences of each religion before and after Abraham's influence.

Chapter 6
Many Religions, One World

What are some of
the differences and
similarities between
religions? Why do
these matter?

Throughout human history, politics, geographic boundaries, and traditions, among other things, have been affected by religion.

During the course of human history, many religions have risen and fallen, each with its own beliefs, rituals, and mythology. Although there are many similarities among religions, there are also many differences. For example, although Judaism, Christianity, and Islam are monotheistic religions, each defines God in a different way. Yet, despite having differences in beliefs and practices, the religions of the world have all had powerful influences on society. They have united some people, divided others, and changed the history of the world.

SPREAD OF RELIGION AROUND THE WORLD

Through time, the major world religions have changed and spread across countries and cultures. In particular, the religions of Buddhism, Christianity, and Islam have spread far from their places of origin.

Christianity began in Jerusalem, but is now practiced on every continent on Earth. Buddhism originated in India, but spread through China and the East. The first followers of Islam lived in Arabia, but today Islam is practiced in many countries. How did this happen? How did these religions transmit their beliefs to so many diverse people in such widespread places?

Several factors help explain how different religions spread so widely. Each faith relied on the work of missionaries and pilgrims to take its message to new people and places. All used relics, which inspired and attracted new followers. A relic is a special object that is treated with great respect because of its connection with a saint, a martyr, or with the past. Religion also has the ability to adapt and incorporate parts of existing cultures and religions into the faith.

After Buddha's death, his followers began to spread his teachings. These monks moved from northern India to the west and east along major trade routes. As they traveled, the monks incorporated the beliefs of the local people into the Buddhist faith. They declared that the local gods had switched to Buddhism. The monks also adopted local worship practices. These adaptations made it easier for people to convert to Buddhism.

> Why is it important for the sustainability of a religion to gain new followers? What happens to religions that never increase their numbers?

FACTS ON FAITH

Relics can be objects owned by spiritual leaders, such as books. Some people find meaning in the body parts of spiritual leaders, including blood, fingers, or even a whole head, and consider those to be relics!

THE SPREAD OF RELIGION

Watch this short video to see how religion has spread around the world. Why does religion spread faster during some periods than others?

🔍 Maps of War history of religion

FACTS ON FAITH

Armies also played a role in the spread of Christianity, with entire conquered populations being baptized into the faith.

MERCHANTS SPREAD CHRISTIANITY

Converts traveled to Jerusalem and returned with holy artifacts and relics. Along the trade routes, relics associated with Jesus and the saints became extremely popular. As merchants carried Christian relics from city to city, they became an important factor in the spread of Christianity beyond the Roman Empire.

The translations of Buddhist texts into other languages also helped spread the religion. Increasingly, people who converted to Buddhism made pilgrimages to India, where Buddha had lived. When they returned to their homelands, they brought back texts and artifacts that became important pieces in the spread of the religion among their own people.

Like Buddhism, Christianity was able to spread to many diverse people and places partly because it was able to adapt to and incorporate local traditions and beliefs. After Jesus's death, scattered groups of Christians spread his message from the Middle East into Europe, Asia, and Africa. When the Roman emperor Constantine declared his conversion to Christianity in 312 CE, the religion spread even farther along the trade routes of Europe, Asia, and North Africa.

[
Christianity's spread was successful because it appealed to many people. Followers embraced the faith's moral standards and the promise of eternal life in heaven.
]

The Islamic religion also spread far and wide from its origins in what many believe to be the city of Mecca in modern-day Saudi Arabia. In just a few years after Muhammad's death in 632, Muslim armies conquered large empires in Eurasia and North Africa. Through time, the people of these lands converted to Islam. The Islamic faith also spread to new lands as missionaries traveled along trade routes. Merchants carried Islam across the Indian Ocean and beyond.

In addition, as more people adopted the Islamic faith and traveled to Islam's holy sites, Muslim pilgrims brought back new teachings and texts to their homes, which helped them spread Islam to even more people.

While Buddhism, Christianity, and Islam spread through missionaries, pilgrims, and converts, other religions, such as Judaism, spread as followers left their homelands and settled in new places. The Jewish diaspora forced Jews to spread throughout the Roman Empire after the Temple of Jerusalem was destroyed in 70 CE. Centuries later, Jewish people live in communities around the world.

THE CRUSADES

Although religion has the power to integrate and unify people of different backgrounds, it can also divide people. Because few things inspire as much devotion and intense feelings as religion, great conflicts can occur between faiths and even within the same faith. Sometimes war and violence have erupted because of religious differences.

The Crusades were a series of military campaigns conducted by European Christians against Muslims in the Middle East during the Middle Ages. In 1076, Muslims had recaptured the holy city of Jerusalem, where Jesus had lived most of his life and where he was crucified. For Christians, there was no holier city on Earth.

At the same time, Muslims viewed Jerusalem as an important site in the Islamic faith, because the prophet Muhammad had spent time in the city. A dome called the Dome of the Rock was built on the site where Muhammad was said to have prayed and from which he ascended. Muslims considered the rock so holy that no human was allowed to touch it.

As these religions spread around the globe, they changed the world around them. At the same time, the religions themselves changed, adapting to and adopting local customs and beliefs.

FACTS ON FAITH

Changes in religion occurred when religious leaders interpreted doctrine in different ways. Other changes occurred when the religion embraced and included local customs and cultures.

For decades, religion has been the source of violent conflict between the countries of India and Pakistan. After the end of British rule in India in 1947, the two countries of India and Pakistan were formed to give followers of Islam in India their own country. This is Pakistan. Conflict between the two countries and between followers of Hinduism and Islam escalated. Since their independence, India and Pakistan have fought three major wars and many smaller skirmishes and battles. The conflict continues today.

FACTS ON FAITH

In Northern Ireland, you can still see walls that were built to separate the Catholic and Protestant communities.

For a period of about 200 years, Christians and Muslims fought over who would control Jerusalem and other areas in the Holy Land. Although the Christians were able to recapture Jerusalem, it was later taken back by the Muslims.

> Today, Jerusalem remains a holy site for Christians, Muslims, and Jews. Because of this, the city is a source of continuing conflict among followers of those faiths.

THE PROTESTANT REFORMATION

While the Crusades were a conflict between followers of two religions, the Protestant Reformation was a conflict that arose within Christianity. By the sixteenth century, the Catholic Church had become powerful and rich and involved in the politics of Western Europe. Some Christians charged the Church with corruption. Members of the Church, such as Martin Luther and John Calvin, called for change and split with the Catholic Church. Martin Luther was even excommunicated.

These men formed their own Protestant religions, which were called Lutheranism and Calvinism. Later, Catholic and Protestant lords and kings used their religious differences as an excuse to fight wars to gain more land and power. The conflict between Protestants and Catholics lasted well into the twentieth century.

ARAB-ISRAELI CONFLICT

The Jewish people spread around the world after being exiled from their homeland in the first century CE. After the Holocaust and World War II, the United Nations General Assembly voted to divide Palestine so that a Jewish national homeland could be created. Muslims already living in the area opposed the plan, and war broke out between the Arab Muslims and Jewish settlers.

Although the 1948 Arab-Israeli War established Israel as an independent state, it did not end the conflict. Many Muslims were forced to leave land that had been in their families for generations and they lost their livelihoods. Many Jews felt the land was theirs to begin with. During the next decades, the two sides, along with their allies in other nations, fought several wars over territory.

Additional conflict has occurred between Israel and the Palestinian people. The Palestinians are a large population of Arab people who were also promised a nation at the end of World War II. When the Israelis arrived in Palestine, the plan for an independent Palestinian state fell apart. Many Palestinians were forced to move to other countries in the Middle East.

In the 1960s, the Palestinian Liberation Organization (PLO) was formed to fight for the rights of Palestinians. The PLO has led violent conflict against Israel as its members fight for a Palestine nation.

Several peace agreements have been made between the Palestinians and the Israelis through the years, but they have always fallen apart with new incidents of violence.

CONFLICT BETWEEN ISLAM AND CHRISTIANITY

Have you heard news stories about Islamic extremists? In recent years, some followers of Islam have come into conflict with the Western Christian world. These followers have extreme ideas about their religion and hold beliefs that can be very different from what the majority of Islamic followers believe. Tension between some Muslims and Christians have led to acts of terrorism and violent conflict between the two sides.

The Golden Rule stresses the importance of caring and compassion for all.

THE GOLDEN RULE

The major religions generally have one overarching principle in common—belief in the Golden Rule. The Golden Rule is a moral code that reflects the idea that every person should treat others as he or she would like to be treated.

> In Christianity, Jesus stated, "Do to others whatever you would have them do to you" (Matthew 7:12). In Buddhism, Buddha has said, "Hurt not others in ways that you yourself would find hurtful" (Udanavarga 5:18).

Although the religions of the world have many differences in beliefs and practices, this simple rule unites all. By focusing on what religions have in common and embracing the Golden Rule, there is hope that the people of the world can find common ground.

KEY QUESTIONS

- **How has history been affected by the spread of different religions?**
- **How would today's world be different without religion?**

FINDING COMMON GROUND BY EXPLORING SIMILARITIES IN WORLD RELIGIONS

While there are many differences among the world's major religions, there are also many similarities. In this activity, you will explore the beliefs, practices, and rituals that build common ground between religions.

* **Based on what you have learned in this book and on any additional research you've done, create a chart that highlights the similarities among religions.** When deciding what information to present, consider the following areas:

    1. Belief in God(s)
    2. Rites and rituals
    3. Sacred texts
    4. Creation stories
    5. Central figures
    6. Central beliefs

* **Which religions have the most similarities?** Which have the fewest? Do your results surprise you?

* **Consider the best format to present what you have learned.** Prepare a chart, graph, or other visual medium to present the results of your research.

* **Compare your results with your friends or classmates.** How do they compare?

> To investigate more, create a map of world religions. Do religions with more similarities share similar geographic locations? Why or why not? How do you think geography plays a role in how a faith has developed?

Inquire & Investigate

MEANING OF THE GOLDEN RULE

Religious historian Karen Armstrong gave a talk about the Golden Rule and what it means to different people. Why do you think the meaning of the Golden Rule changes?

PS

🔍 "Karen Armstrong" Golden Rule

I GOD   BLUE GODS   SYMBOL

2+ GODS   RBIDDEN FOODS

RESEARCH AN HISTORICAL CONFLICT OVER RELIGION

In this activity, you will choose a historical religious conflict and research it to learn more about its causes and effects.

- **Choose a historical religious conflict that you want to learn more about.** You can pick one discussed in this chapter or another conflict.

- **Research the conflict online or at the library.** Consider the following questions.

  1. Where did the conflict take place?

  2. What did each side hope to gain? Why was that important to it?

  3. What do you think life is like for a person living in this region during this time?

  4. How was the conflict resolved? Is it still ongoing? How would you propose to solve this conflict?

- **Create a peace plan that you will present to both sides in this conflict.** Explain your plan and why you believe it is fair for both sides.

> To investigate more, think about the values and morals taught by the religions involved in the conflict. How does each side's actions support or contradict its religion?

HMM...

BRIDGING THE GAP

Throughout history, people of different religions have sometimes regarded each other with distrust and fear. Many times, this fear comes from a lack of understanding about a religion and its beliefs and practices. For example, many non-Muslims in Europe and the United States fear people who practice Islam, even though Islam is a peaceful religion. In this activity, you will investigate ways to promote understanding between people of different religious faiths.

- **Think about the ways misunderstandings arise between followers of different religions.** Choose two religions in conflict, such as Christian/Muslim, Hindu/Buddhist, Muslim/Jew. What differences exist that have created gaps in understanding between these two religions? What is the point of view of a person from each side?

- **Think about ways that you could promote understanding and reduce animosity between people of the two religions.** Come up with at least three proposals.

- **Write a brief essay that explains your plan to bridge the gap between religions.** Be sure to include an introductory paragraph, separate paragraphs for each of your three main points, and a conclusion.

- **Share your essay with your class.**

To investigate more, think about conflicts that are not considered religious, such as the First and Second World Wars. Did religion play any role in these conflicts? How do you know?

I DON'T THINK THAT JUST SAYING "SORRY" IS GONNA CUT IT....

THANKS FOR THE HELP!

JUST DOING MY MORAL DUTY!

To investigate more, consider that some people do not believe in the existence of any gods and do not follow any religion. These people are called atheists. How might this point of view influence behavior? Discuss this topic with a person who does not believe in religion. What influences their behavior?

RELIGION AND BEHAVIOR

Does religion influence behavior? Most people would say yes. All religions have a moral code, which gives followers rules and standards to live by. In this activity, you will investigate the connection between religion and behavior.

- **Read the following article.** How do you think religion influenced the behavior of the football players in this article?

Deseret News football "Carson Jones"

- **Now think about your own religion.** What are the moral codes of your religion? How do you put them into practice in your own life? Give examples.

- **Have you ever been intimidated by peer pressure from other people to ignore your religious ideals?** Did you modify your behavior? Explain.

- **Talk to people from different religions.** How do they put the moral codes from their faith into practice? In what ways do they believe religion has influenced their behavior? How has peer pressure influenced their behavior and following of religious ideals?

- **Consider how the nature of different Gods influences behavior.** Read this article from researchers at the University of Oregon. Do you agree or disagree with the findings in this article? Why or why not?

Oregon religion influences behavior

- **Write a brief essay that explains how you think religion influences behavior.** Be sure to include an introductory paragraph, separate paragraphs for each of your three main points, and a conclusion.

- **Share your essay with your class.**

adaptation: the act of adjusting.

adultery: unfaithfulness of a married man or woman.

afterlife: an existence after death.

Allah: the name of God in Islam.

allegory: the use of symbolic figures and actions to express truths about the human experience.

alms: something given freely to help the poor.

altar: a large table in house of worship that is used in religious ceremonies.

ambiguity: being able to be understood in more than one way.

angel: a messenger of God in some religions.

anoint: the rubbing of oil on a person's head during a religious ceremony.

anti-Semitism: hostility toward people who practice Judaism.

apostles: Jesus's 12 original disciples in Christianity.

ark: in Judaism, a cabinet in which the Torah scrolls are kept.

artifact: an object made or changed by human beings in the past, such as a tool or weapon.

ascetic: a person who lives a strict and simple life and often practices extreme self-denial for religious purposes.

ashrama: in Hinduism, one of the four age-based life stages.

atman: the individual soul in Hinduism.

atone: to make amends.

austerity: to live simply with few luxuries or comforts.

baptism: the sacrament that admits a person into the Christian faith and involves being sprinkled with or immersed in water.

bar mitzvah: a ceremony marking a boy's transition to adulthood in the Jewish faith.

bat mitzvah: a ceremony marking a girl's transition to adulthood in the Jewish faith.

BCE: put after a date, BCE stands for Before Common Era and counts years down to zero. CE stands for Common Era and counts years up from zero. This book was published in 2015 CE.

belief: a principle or idea that is accepted as the truth.

Bible: the sacred text of Christianity.

bimah: a platform in a Jewish synagogue that holds the reading table used when chanting or reading from the Torah.

blasphemy: the act of saying offensive things about a religion or God.

bodhisattva: a person in the process of becoming a Buddha, who puts off final enlightenment to help others on the path to enlightenment.

Brahma: the Hindu creator god.

Brahman: the divine and transcendent power that exists beyond the universe in Hinduism.

Brahmins: priests and intellectuals who perform religious rituals and are the highest of the four major classes of Hindu society.

Buddha: an enlightened being in the Buddhist faith.

Buddhism: a religion based on the teachings of Buddha.

Buddhist: a follower of Buddhism.

caliph: a political and religious leader in Islam.

cantor: a person who sings and leads people in prayer in a church or temple.

Catholicism: a branch of Christianity.

ceremony: a series of formal acts in a ritual.

chancel: a part of a church near the altar, often reserved for the clergy and choir.

Christian: a follower of Christianity.

Christianity: the world's largest religion, whose followers believe that Jesus Christ is the son of God.

circumcise: the surgical removal of the foreskin from a human male's penis.

clergy: a priest, monk, minister, or other person ordained by the church.

commandment: a divine rule from God.

communion: a sacrament in which some Christian denominations consecrate and share bread and wine during a religious service.

conceive: to become pregnant.

confirmation: a sacrament in which some Christian denominations confirm their faith.

conquest: the use of military force to take control of land and its people.

GLOSSARY

consecrate: to declare something blessed or holy.

conservative: following traditional values and attitudes.

convert: to change to a different religion.

corruption: dishonest actions by those in power.

cosmology: the science of the origin and development of the universe.

covenant: a formal and serious agreement or promise.

covet: to desire to have something.

craving: an intense desire for something, such as a particular food.

creation: the act of causing something to exist.

cremate: to burn the body of a person who has died.

criteria: the standard by which something is judged or measured.

crucifixion: a slow and painful execution in which a person is tied or nailed to a large wooden cross and left to hang until death.

cultural: relating to the behaviors, beliefs, and way of life of a group of people.

Dalai Lama: the spiritual head of Tibetan Buddhism.

debate: a discussion between people with differing viewpoints.

deity: a god or goddess.

denomination: a religious group.

descend: to move from a higher place to a lower place.

design: to plan for a particular purpose or to plan artistically.

devotion: a form of prayer or worship for special use.

dharma: the moral path that a person must follow.

diaspora: the movement of Jewish people to countries outside of Israel.

disciple: a follower of a religious leader, who spreads their teachings.

discriminate: to unfairly treat a person or group differently from others, usually because of who they are.

divine: related to a god.

diya: an oil lamp, usually made from clay, that is used in Hindu festivals and ceremonies.

doctrine: a set of beliefs held by a religious group.

dukkha: a Buddhist term for suffering.

duty: something that one is expected or required to do.

Eastern Orthodoxy: a branch of Christianity.

eid: a Muslim term for festival or holiday.

eightfold: eight times.

empire: a large state or group of states that is ruled by a single ruler called an emperor.

enlightenment: the discovery of the ultimate truth of life.

era: a period of time with certain characteristics.

eternal: everlasting or perpetual.

eternity: lasting forever.

ethics: relating to good and evil and moral duties.

Eucharist: a sacrament in Christianity that involves taking bread and wine as the body and blood of Christ.

excommunicate: to officially exclude someone from participating in the sacraments and religious services of the Christian Church.

extremist: a person who holds extreme or fanatical political or religious views.

faith: strong religions feeling and belief in God.

famine: an extreme shortage of food.

fasting: not eating or drinking by choice for a period of time as part of a religious ritual.

feminine: having qualities that are usually associated with women.

Four Noble Truths: the central teachings of Buddhism that explain the nature of suffering, its causes, and how to overcome it.

fundamentalist: a religious view in which a person rigidly follows fundamental principles.

God: the Supreme Being, creator and ruler of the universe.

Gospels: the four books of the Bible's New Testament that document Jesus's life and teachings.

guru: a teacher.

Hadith: accounts of the prophet Muhammad's actions and teachings.

hafiz: a person who has completely memorized the Islamic Qur'an.

hajj: a pilgrimage to Mecca and one of the pillars of Islam.

Hasidism: a Jewish movement founded in eighteenth-century Eastern Europe.

hijab: a court official in Islam.

Hindu: a follower of Hinduism.

Hinduism: a group of religious beliefs, traditions, and practices from South Asia.

Holocaust: the systematic murder and persecution of Jewish people by the German Nazi state.

holy: sacred.

homosexual: a person who is sexually attracted to others of the same gender.

humility: having a modest opinion of oneself.

hygiene: practices that keep things clean and prevent the spread of germs.

hymn: a religious song written for praise and worship.

idolatry: the worship of idols.

imam: a leader of prayers in a mosque or one of the leaders of the Shi'a Muslim community.

immortal: someone who will not die.

impermanence: not lasting.

incarnation: the belief that Jesus Christ was both divine and human. Also one of a series of lives that a person is believed to have had in the past in Hinduism.

inevitable: unable to be avoided.

insight: the ability to see into and understand a situation.

interconnected: being related to one another.

interfaith: involving people of different religions.

invaders: people who enter another land to raid and conquer it.

Islam: a monotheistic religion developed in the Middle East that follows the teachings of the prophet Muhammad.

jihad: a Muslim religious duty to struggle against evil, either spiritually or physically.

Jew: a person whose religion is Judaism.

Judaism: a monotheistic religion that uses the Torah as its sacred text.

kamya: an optional Hindu ritual such as a pilgrimage.

karma: the law of moral cause and effect that influences reincarnation in Hinduism and Buddhism.

kosher: adhering to Jewish dietary laws.

kshatriya: a member of the Hindu royal and warrior class.

leader: a person who guides and directs others in a group.

leavened: risen dough.

liberal: the belief in individual freedoms and reform.

liberation: the act of being freed from oppression and gaining equal rights and opportunities.

luminescent: the emission of light.

magga: the end of suffering and one of the Four Noble Truths of Buddhism.

mandala: a sacred diagram used as a focus for mediation and other rituals in Buddhism.

manifestation: an outward appearance, display, or demonstration.

mantra: a word or phrase repeated, chanted, or sung as a prayer.

martyr: a person who endures great suffering and death for his or her religious beliefs.

meditation: religious thought and spiritual introspection.

menorah: a candelabrum with nine branches that is used in the Jewish festival of Hanukkah.

messiah: a promised savior and deliverer.

Messianic Age: a future time where there is peace on Earth and no crime, poverty, or war.

metaphor: the comparison of one thing to another without using the words *like* or *as*.

Middle Ages: the period of time between the end of the Roman Empire and the Renaissance, about 350 to 1450 CE.

Middle East: the countries of Southwest Asia and North Africa, from Libya in the west to Afghanistan in the east.

mindfulness: the intentional focus of one's attention on emotions and sensations in the present moment.

ministry: a period of service as a minister.

minyan: a group of 10 Jewish adults required for certain religious obligations and rituals.

miracle: an unusual or wonderful event that is believed to be caused by the power of God.

GLOSSARY

missionary: a member of a religious group that is sent into another area to spread the word about his or her religion's teachings and perform works of service.

mitzvah: a Hebrew word that means commandment.

moksha: release from the cycle of birth and death in Hinduism.

monk: a member of a religious community of men that typically takes vows of poverty, chastity, and obedience.

monotheism: the belief in one, all-powerful God.

moral: relating to right and wrong behavior and character.

mosque: a place of worship for followers of Islam.

muezzin: a man who calls Muslims to prayer in a mosque.

murti: an image or representation of a divine spirit, such as in stone, clay, or wood.

Muslim: a person who follows the religion of Islam.

mythology: the collected myths of a group of people.

naimittika: a Sanskrit word meaning incidental, a group of rituals in Hinduism that are performed when a particular occasion occurs, such as the birth of a child.

narrative: a spoken or written story of events.

Nativity: birth, often refers to the birth of Jesus in Christianity.

nave: the central part of a church building.

nirodha: one of the Four Noble Truths of Buddhism, the end of suffering.

nirvana: the state of liberation from the cycle of death and rebirth.

nitya: daily religious rituals in Hinduism.

noble: an exalted moral or mental character.

oral tradition: traditions passed on from one generation to the next by word of mouth.

ordain: a religious ceremony that makes a person a member of the clergy who can perform religious rites and ceremonies.

orthodox: following traditional and accepted religious norms.

pantheistic: a religious belief that identifies God with the universe.

parable: a short story designed to teach or illustrate religious beliefs and moral lessons.

parchment: the skin of an animal that is prepared in a way that it can be written on.

patriarch: a man who controls a family, group, or government.

penance: a sacrament in Christianity in which a person confesses and atones for his or her sins.

persecution: a campaign to exterminate or drive away a group of people based on their religious beliefs or other characteristic.

philosophy: the study of truth, wisdom, the nature of reality, and knowledge.

pilgrimage: a trip to visit a holy site.

pillar: a column that supports a part of a building or a basic fact, idea, or principle of something.

plague: a serious disease that spreads quickly to many people and often cause death.

polytheistic: the belief in many gods.

pope: the head of the Catholic Church.

prayer: an appeal or thanks to God.

precept: a guide or rule for moral behavior.

prestige: having or showing rank, success, or wealth.

priest: a member of the clergy in Christianity that leads religious services and performs rites.

prophet: a person who is believed to speak for God.

Protestantism: a branch of Christianity.

pulpit: a raised platform in a church where clergy stand to speak to followers.

purification: the process of making something clean and pure.

purify: to make something clean and pure.

Qur'an: the sacred text of Islam.

rabbi: a Jewish teacher and spiritual leader.

Ramadan: a month of fasting in Islam to commemorate the time when Muhammad received his first revelations from God.

rangoli: a colorful Indian decorative pattern made on the floor near the entrance to welcome guests.

realm: kingdom.

rebirth: to be born again.

reform: to change something for the better.

reincarnation: the belief that after death, the soul comes back to Earth in another body or form.

relic: an object that belonged to a saint or other holy person.

religious: practicing a specific system of beliefs through worship, obedience, and prayer.

resurrection: the rising of Jesus from the dead in Christianity.

revelation: a surprising fact that is made known.

reverence: great respect and love.

righteousness: being morally right or justified.

rite: an act in a religious ceremony.

ritual: a set of actions that is always performed in the same way as part of a religious ceremony.

Sabbath: the day of rest and worship. In the Jewish faith, the Sabbath occurs from sunset on Friday to sunset on Saturday, while the Christian Sabbath is on Sunday.

sacraments: rituals in Christianity.

sacred: something that is holy.

sacrifice: to give up something to benefit another.

saint: a person honored by the Christian church because of their holy life.

salat: prayer and the second pillar of Islam.

salvation: being saved from

sin, evil, harm, or destruction.

samsara: the cycle of rebirth in Hinduism and Buddhism.

samudaya: the origin of suffering and one of the Four Noble Truths of Buddhism.

Sanskrit: the primary language of Hinduism.

savior: one who saves others from danger. In Christianity, Jesus is believed to be the savior of souls.

sawm: fasting and the fourth pillar of Islam.

scholar: a person with a great deal of knowledge.

scribe: a person who copies books, letters, and other documents by hand.

scripture: a sacred book.

scroll: a piece of paper or parchment with writing on it that is rolled up into the shape of a tube.

sect: a group whose members share the same beliefs and practices.

seder: a Jewish ritual that involves the retelling of the story of the escape of the Israelites from slavery in ancient Egypt.

segregate: to keep apart.

sermon: a speech given by a member of the clergy during a religious service.

shahada: the first and most important pillar of Islam, which professes the Muslim belief that there is only one God and Muhammad is his prophet.

Shakti: the feminine form of the divine in Hinduism.

Shi'a: one of the two main groups of Muslims.

shiva: in Judaism, a week-long period of mourning for relatives who have passed away.

Shiva Nataraja: one of the forms of the Hindu god Shiva as the Lord of the Dance.

shramana: a religious ascetic in Buddhism.

shrine: a sacred or holy place that is dedicated to a specific deity, martyr, or saint.

shroud: a length of cloth in which a dead person is wrapped and buried.

shruti: meaning that which is heard, and is used to describe the four Vedas of Hinduism.

shudra: the fourth and lowest varna, or social class, of Hinduism.

sin: the act of disobeying God's will.

smriti: meaning that which has been remembered, and is used to describe the four Vedas of Hinduism.

soul: the eternal or real self.

spiritual: relating to the mind and spirit instead of the physical world.

stupa: a burial mound that contains ashes or relics of Buddha.

submission: the act of obeying another person or force.

sunna: the teachings, actions, and saying of the Islamic prophet Muhammad that are passed down orally from one generation to the next.

Sunni: one of the two main groups of Muslims.

GLOSSARY

supernatural: unable to be explained by science or the laws of nature.

supreme: the highest rank or authority.

sustainability: the ability to endure.

symbolic: something that stands for or represents something else.

synagogue: a place where Jewish people worship and study.

tallit: a prayer shawl worn by Jewish men.

Talmud: a text that contains discussion and interpretations of the Torah, Judaism's sacred text.

tamid: a sanctuary lamp in a Jewish temple that is usually located in front of the ark where the Torah scrolls are located.

tenet: a principle or belief that is held to be true.

terrorism: the use of violence and threats to frighten people.

testament: one of two main sections of the Christian Bible.

tolerance: the willingness to respect or accept the customs, beliefs, or opinions of others.

Torah: the first five books of the Hebrew Bible, which represent the teachings given to Moses by God.

tradition: the handing down of customs, ideas, and beliefs from one generation to the next.

transcendent: having continuous existence outside the created world.

transept: the part of a church or other building that lies across the main body of the building at right angles.

transgression: an act that goes against laws or rules.

treason: the crime of betraying one's country.

Trimurti: the ruling trio of gods in Hinduism: Brahma, Vishnu, and Shiva.

Trinity: the Christian concept of three forms of a single God: Father, Son, and Holy Spirit.

upanayana: a Hindu ritual which marks a male child's initiation into the life of a student and acceptance as a full member of the religious community.

Upanishads: one of the sacred texts of Hinduism.

vaisha: one of the four classes, or varnas, of Hindu society.

varnas: the classes of Hindu society.

vaulted: an arched structure.

Vedas: one of the sacred texts of Hinduism.

virgin: a person who has not had sexual intercourse.

virtue: any good quality or trait.

Vishnu: one of the three ruling gods of Hinduism, known as the Preserver.

wheel of life: the endless cycle of birth, death, and rebirth in Buddhism.

worship: to express love or devotion to God.

yantras: Hindu diagrams of the universe.

yarmulke: a skullcap worn by many Jewish men.

yoga: a form of physical and mental exercise and mediation.

zakat: paying of charity and the third pillar of Islam.

Zionism: a political movement to establish a national homeland for the Jewish people in Palestine, and the development of the modern state of Israel.

RESOURCES

⊙ BOOKS

Ambalu, Shulamit. *The Religions Book: Big Ideas Simply Explained.* New York: DK, 2013.

Bowker, John. *World Religions: The Great Faiths Explored & Explained*. New York: DK, 2006.

Cooke, Tim. *National Geographic Concise History of World Religions: An Illustrated Time Line*. Washington, D.C.: National Geographic, 2011.

⊙ WEBSITES

Religion Facts: www.religionfacts.com, This website has many facts about a variety of world religions.

Internet Sacred Text Archive: www.sacred-texts.com/about.htm, This website is a free archive of electronic texts about religion and other topics and includes the sacred texts of several religions.

Sacred Texts: www.bl.uk/learning/cult/sacredbooks/sacredintro.html, This website from the British Library has interactive exhibits that allow readers to watch animated stories from several sacred texts as well as listen to a panel of experts answer questions about the texts.

The United Religions Initiative (URI): www.uri.org/kids/index.htm, This website has information about several major world religions that readers can explore.

⊙ QR CODE GLOSSARY

Page 13: whc.unesco.org/en/list/244/gallery

Page 17: www.youtube.com/watch?v=u15lCz2U0lU
• www.youtube.com/watch?v=Yiupwfu_h0k •
www.templenet.com/Articles/hintemp.html

Page 24: www.youtube.com/watch?v=VI-BbATfLXo
• www.youtube.com/playlist?list=PLui6Eyny-
UzyugJTu3l1YFL0k3nGIlaz9

Page 28: www.ibiblio.org/expo/deadsea.
scrolls.exhibit/intro.html

Page 38: www.youtube.com/watch?v=4kE8W5xEe88

Page 40: www.chabad.org/library/article_cdo/aid/246616/
jewish/The-Great-Test-The-Binding-of-Isaac.htm

Page 41: www.chabad.org/library/bible_cdo/aid/9992

Page 52: buddhismnow.com/2013/04/15/buddhist-wheel-
of-life • buddhism.about.com/od/tibetandeities/
ig/Wheel-of-Life-Gallery/Bhavachakra.htm

Page 54: www.dharmanet.org/lcsutrastherv.htm

Page 56: www.buddhanet.net/audio-chant.htm

Page 57: www.mymodernmet.com/profiles/
blogs/tibetan-buddhist-monks-sand-art

Page 58: www.youtube.com/watch?v=txujqGtR_6g
• whc.unesco.org/en/list/592

Page 59: www.youtube.com/watch?v=qk-9Ez3xICY

Page 61: www.dalailama.com •
www.youtube.com/user/gyalwarinpoche •
www.gluckman.com/DalaiLama.html

Page 72: www.santuario-fatima.pt/portal/index.
php?id=1000 • en.lourdes-france.org

Page 78: www.cathedral.org/visit/onlineTours.shtml

Page 79: www.biblegateway.com/
passage/?search=Luke%2010:25-37

Page 80: www.biblegateway.com/passage/?search=Gene
sis+1&version=GNT •
www.youtube.com/watch?v=Y9yWwFWpbRo •
www.youtube.com/watch?v=qansyCThC_k

Page 87: www.noblequran.com/translation

Page 88: video.nationalgeographic.com/
video/saudiarabia_mecca

Page 96: www.youtube.com/watch?v=ocyyxHkCvm8 •
www.khanacademy.org/humanities/art-islam/beginners-
guide-islamic/a/introduction-to-mosque-architecture
• www.tourmakerturkey.com/blue-mosque.html

Page 97: www.ahadees.com/english-surah-19.html •
www.biblegateway.com/passage/?search=Luke%20
2:1-35 • www.biblegateway.com/
passage/?search=Luke+1%3A26-37&version=NASB

Page 98: hwww.noblequran.com/translation •
jewishvirtuallibrary.org/jsource/Bible/Genesis22.
html • www.kingjamesbibleonline.org/book.ph
p?book=Genesis&chapter=22&verse=&t=1

Page 101: www.mapsofwar.com/ind/
history-of-religion.html

Page 107: www.youtube.com/watch?v=bhHJ4DRZNZM

Page 110: www.deseretnews.com/article/865566351/
Kindness-of-Arizona-high-school-QB-Carson-Jones-
and-teammates-has-gone-viral.html?pg=all • around.
uoregon.edu/content/researcher-religion-influences-
behavior-%E2%80%94-both-good-and-bad

INDEX

A

Abraham, vi, 27–28, 40, 82, 83, 84, 93, 98
activities (Inquire & Investigate)
    Architecture and Mosques, 96
    Architecture and the National Cathedral in Washington, DC, 78
    Bridging the Gap, 109
    Compare Buddhism and Hinduism in a Venn Diagram, 60
    Compare Creation Stories, 80
    Comparing Abraham in Three Sacred Texts, 98
    Create a Sand Mandala, 62
    Explore the Dalai Lama's Teachings, 61
    Finding Common Ground by Exploring Similarities in World Religions, 107
    Finding Facts in Sacred Text, 41
    Interpret a Parable, 79
    Interview a Muslim Imam, a Jewish Rabbi, and a Christian Priest or Minister, 95
    Interview a Person of the Hindu Faith, 22–23
    Practice Yoga, 24
    Religion and Behavior, 110
    Research an Historical Conflict Over Religion, 108
    Sacred Text: The Story of Abraham and Isaac, 40
    Understanding Sacred Texts: the Qur'an and the Christian Bible, 97
    Unleavened Bread for Passover, 42
    What Is Religion?, 6
afterlife beliefs, vi, 3, 10–11, 47, 67, 68, 70–71, 91, 92

B

Bible, 4, 40–41, 64–65, 70, 71–72, 97, 98
Buddhism
    branches of, vi, 51
    cycle of rebirth in, 47, 52, 53
    Dalai Lama as spiritual leader in, vii, 58–59, 61
    Five Precepts of, 55
    Four Noble Truths of, 47, 48–49
    Golden Rule in, 106
    meditation and prayer in, 46, 50, 54, 55, 56–57
    Noble Eightfold Path in, 49, 50
    number of followers of, 44
    origin of the universe in, 53
    origins of, vi, 44, 45–46, 60
    Pali Canon/sacred texts in, vi, 54, 102
    personal development in, 53–54
    rituals and celebrations, 57
    shrines and temples in, 56, 57, 58
    spread of, vii, 51, 100–102, 103
    wheel of life in, 51–52
    worship in, 56–57

C

ceremonies/celebrations, 4, 18, 19, 36, 38–39, 42, 57, 75, 76–77, 89, 91–93
Christianity
    afterlife beliefs in, vi, 3, 67, 68, 70–71
    Bible/sacred text in, 4, 64–65, 70, 71–72, 97, 98
    branches/denominations of, vii, 70, 72–75, 76, 104
    churches in, 73, 75–76, 78

crucifixion and resurrection in, vi, 66–67, 76, 77
The Crusades based on, vii, 103–104
discrimination and persecution based on, 67, 68
Golden Rule in, 106
holidays and celebrations in, 75, 76–77
Holy Trinity in, 68–69
Islamic conflicts with, 103–104, 105
Jesus of Nazareth in, vi, 33, 64–67, 68–70, 74–75, 76–77, 79, 82, 97, 102, 103
number of followers of, 64, 77
prayer and worship in, 70, 73–75
Protestant Reformation in, 73, 104
rituals/rites in, 74–75
salvation in, 70–71
spread of, 67–68, 100–102, 103
supreme being/God in, 68–69
Ten Commandments in, 4, 69
churches, 73, 75–76, 78. *See also* mosques; temples
creation stories, 4, 5, 13, 53, 80
The Crusades, vii, 103–104

D

Dalai Lama, vii, 58–59, 61
discrimination and persecution, vii, 34, 39, 67, 68, 85, 105

F

festivals. *See* ceremonies/celebrations
food/feasts/fasting, 4, 35, 36, 42, 76–77, 88, 89, 91–92

INDEX

P

Pali Canon, vi, 54
pilgrimages, 4, 17–18, 47, 49, 56, 72, 88, 89–90, 102–103
prayer/meditation, 4, 33–34, 36, 46, 50, 54, 55, 56–57, 70, 73–75, 84, 88, 89, 90–91, 92
Protestant Reformation, 73, 104

Q

Qur'an, vii, 4, 84, 85, 87–88, 92, 97, 98

R

Ramadan, 88, 89, 91–92
reincarnation, 10–11, 14, 47, 50
relics, 47, 101, 102
religion
    Buddhism as, vi, vii, 15, 44–62, 100–102, 103, 106
    Christianity as, vi, vii, 3, 4, 33, 64–80, 82, 97, 98, 100–101, 102, 103–104, 105, 106
    definition and description of, 2–6
    differences and commonalities among, 3–5, 100–110
    Hinduism as, vi, 3, 5, 8–24, 53, 60, 80, 104
    Islam as, vii, 4, 82–98, 100–101, 102–104, 105
    Judaism as, vi, vii, 4, 26–42, 65, 66, 71, 82, 98, 103, 105
    monotheistic, 3, 12, 27, 68–69, 82 *See also* supreme being/God
    number of followers of, 5, 9, 26, 44, 64, 77, 83, 86

polytheistic, 3, 12
spread of, vii, 27, 51, 67–68, 86, 100–103
timeline of, vi–vii
rituals/rites, 4, 12, 17–18, 20, 21, 37, 57, 74–75, 91. *See also* pilgrimages; sacrifices

S

sacred texts, vi, vii, 4, 9, 13, 14–16, 30, 31–32, 34–35, 36, 40–41, 54, 64–65, 70, 71–72, 84, 85, 87–88, 92, 97, 98, 102
sacrifices, 21, 28, 53, 77, 91–92, 93
salvation, 3, 70–71
shrines, 16, 17, 56
supreme being/God, 11, 12, 14, 26, 27, 29, 68–69, 82–83, 85, 88
synagogues, vi, 33–34, 37

T

temples, vi, 17, 33–34, 37, 57, 58. *See also* churches
Ten Commandments, 4, 30, 69
Torah, vi, 30, 31–32, 34–35, 36, 41

V

Vedas, vi, 9, 13, 14–16

W

women, religious views of, 21, 34, 36, 72, 73, 84, 91
worship, 4, 16–17, 33–34, 36, 56–57, 73–75, 90–91

Y

yoga, 18–19, 24

Z

Zionism, 34